Microsoft®
Word 2013:
Level 2 of 3

JILL MURPHY

Custom Performance Solutions

LABYRINTH

LEARNING™

Berkeley, CA

Microsoft Word 2013: Level 2

LABYRINTH

LEARNING™

Labyrinth Learning
2560 9th Street, Suite 320
Berkeley, California 94710
800.522.9746
On the web at lablearning.com

President:
Brian Favro

Product Development Manager:
Jason Favro

Managing Editor:
Laura Popelka

Production Editor:
Margaret Young

Production Manager:
Rad Proctor

eLearning Production Manager:
Arl S. Nadel

eLearning Development:
Judy Mardar and Andrew Vaughnley

Developmental Editors:
Trisha Conlon and Sandra Rittman

Indexing:
Joanne Sprott

Cover Design:
Mick Koller, SuperLab Design

Interior Design:
Mark Ong, Side-by-Side Studio

ITEM: 1-59136-489-2
ISBN-13: 978-1-59136-489-4

Manufactured in the United States of America.

10 9 8 7 6 5 4 3 2 1

Table of Contents

WORD 2013 LESSON 9:
CREATING A PROMOTIONAL BROCHURE AND A FORM

Quick Reference Tables

Preface

In today's digital world, knowing how to use the most popular suite of desktop software applications is critical. Our goal is to teach new users how to take advantage of this technology and to help experienced users understand how the applications have changed from previous versions. We begin with fundamental concepts and take learners through a systematic progression of exercises, resulting in skill mastery.

An online student resource center accompanies this book. It contains Concepts Review quizzes, student exercise files, and other learning tools. The URL for the student resource center is printed on the inside front cover of this textbook.

Supplemental Options

Video Tutorials: Our easy-to-follow instructional design is complemented with hundreds of videos that demonstrate the concepts and skills covered in this textbook. All videos can be accessed online with a single license key. Videos are an option for all learners. Keys can be purchased at http://lablearning.com/Store/Shop-Videos.

eLab Course Management System: eLab is a web-based learning systems that integrates seamlessly with this textbook. eLab is an option for students enrolled in instructor-led courses that have adopted eLab as part of their course curriculum.

Visual Conventions

This book uses visual and typographic cues to guide students through the lessons. Some of these cues are described below.

`Type this text`	Text you type at the keyboard is printed in this typeface.
Action words	The important action words in exercise steps are presented in boldface.
Ribbon	Glossary terms are presented in black text with a blue background.
	Tips, notes, and warnings are called out with special icons.
Command→ Command→ Command→ Command	Commands to execute from the Ribbon are presented like this: Ribbon Tab→Command Group→Command→Subcommand.
FROM THE KEYBOARD Ctrl+S to save	These margin notes present shortcut keys for executing certain tasks.
FROM THE RIBBON File→Save	These margin notes show Ribbon paths for executing certain tasks.

Acknowledgements

This textbook has benefited greatly from the reviews and suggestions of the following instructors.

Kim Anderson, *Elgin Community College*

Ann Blackman, *Parkland College*

Kristen Bogue, *Bridgerland Applied Technology College*

Jeanann Boyce, *Montgomery College, Takoma Park Campus, MD*

Margie Brunson, *Central Carolina Technical College*

Lori Collins, *Pike-Lincoln Technical Center*

Julie Davis, *Mt. Diablo Adult Ed (Loma Vista Adult School)*

Evangelina Galelgos-Garner, *South Texas Vocational Technical Institute*

Teresita Galvizo, *South East High School*

Rebecca Haney, *Isothermal Community College*

Holly Heggestad, *Madison Area Technical College*

Kathleen Holliman, *Wallace Community College Selma*

Terri Holly, *Indian River State College*

Joan Johnson, *Lake Sumter Community College*

Ronald Kaufer, *Lonestar College – Tomball*

Robin Landry, *RPCC/TEC*

Gayle Larson, *Highline Community College*

Teresa Loftis, *San Bernardino Adult School*

Tina Mazuch, *Northeast Community College*

John Mims, *Central New Mexico Community College Workforce Training Center*

Sue Mookram, *Plaza College and Queens College*

Kay Nelson, *The Lifelong Learning Center, Missoula County Public Schools*

Youcef Oubraham, *HCCC*

Monika Olsen, *Acalanes Adult Education*

Kari Phillips, *DATC*

Kate Prussing, *SERRC – The Learning Connection*

Teresa Roberts, *Wilson Community College*

Maryla Scarpa, *Vincennes University Jasper*

Rosemarie Shamieh, *Glendale Community College*

Lal Shimpi, *Saint Augustine's University*

Mary Jo Slater, *Community College of Beaver County*

Francine Smith, *Wayne Community College*

Michelle Vlaich-Lee, *Greenville Technical College*

Cynthia Wade, *CierraTEC*

Deanna Wallace, *TTC Nashville*

Ali Ware, *Humboldt County Office of Education*

Microsoft® Word 2013:
Level 2 of 3

Creating a Research Paper

LEARNING OBJECTIVES

After studying this lesson, you will be able to:

- Insert footnotes, endnotes, and citations
- Generate a bibliography
- Insert captions and a table of figures
- Create templates

In this lesson, you will learn about research papers, a requirement for nearly every undergraduate and graduate student, and for many professionally employed individuals. You will use Word to develop a research paper using widely accepted style conventions. Your paper will include footnotes, citations, and a table of figures. Then you will create a research paper template to simplify writing future research papers.

Researching Internet Commerce

Green Clean is a successful environmentally conscious janitorial service company. You are the administrative assistant at Green Clean while continuing with your undergraduate work in marketing. You were assigned the task of writing a research paper. The main topic must be on Internet commerce, and since you are also interested in the environment, you put your own spin on the paper to include what effect ecommerce has had on the environment.

You use Word to set up the research paper. Following Modern Language Association (MLA) guidelines, you use footnotes, citations, and captions. You find that the Bibliography and Table of Figures features make it easy to organize reference information in your paper.

Simpson 2

Brian Simpson

Professor Williams

Marketing 222

May 10, 2013

Internet Commerce and Its Effect on the Environment

The Internet had its origins in the 1960s when the Department of Defense developed a communications network to connect the computers of various military installations. The Department of Defense removed its computers from this network in the 1980s and turned over the control to the National Science Foundation (NSF). In 1992, the U.S. government withdrew funding from the NSF and encouraged private companies to administer and control the "Internet." It was at this point that Internet commerce was born. Companies both large and small suddenly realized the enormous marketing potential of this global computer network. In fact, by 2007 the Internet had no doubt become the largest global marketplace.[1]

The commercial potential of the Internet stems from the fact that it is a global network with inexpensive access.[2] The Internet is also available 24x7. The multimedia capability to the Internet is important for marketing and advertising. Quick product delivery, automated order-taking, and low overhead are several more factors that are driving Internet commerce.[3]

---

[1] This is the opinion of many business leaders and economists.

[2] This is true in the United States, but some nations still have high rates due to limited competition among Internet service providers.

[3] These factors depend upon the capabilities of individual companies.

Using Research Paper Styles

Video Library   http://labyrinthelab.com/videos   Video Number: WD13-V0601

There are several documentation styles, each with their own specific formatting requirements. The MLA style has been the standard for undergraduate and graduate research papers for many years.

Understanding the MLA Documentation Style

The MLA publishes the *Modern Language Association Handbook for Writers of Research Papers*. The MLA style has very specific formatting requirements, *some* of which are already defaults within Microsoft Word. For example, Word's default margins are one inch, which complies with the MLA requirement. However, Word does not comply with *all* MLA guidelines by default.

This lesson does not presume to be a resource for MLA guidelines. Refer to the MLA handbook or MLA website (http://mla.org) for guidance in complying with MLA requirements.

Following is an overview of *some* of the MLA style guidelines.

Student name and the page number on every page at one-half inch from the top.

The student name, professor, course, and date lines are positioned here.

Brian Simpson

Professor Williams

Marketing 222

May 10, 2013

The title of the paper follows the date line.

Internet Commerce and Its Effect on the Environment

The Internet had its origins in the 1960s when the Department of Defense developed a communications network to connect the computers of various military installations. The Department of Defense removed its computers from this network in the 1980s and turned over the control to the National Science Foundation (NSF). In 1992, the U.S. government withdrew funding from the NSF and encouraged private companies to administer and control the "Internet." It was at this point that Internet commerce was born. Companies both large and small suddenly realized the enormous marketing potential of this global computer network. In fact, by 2007 the Internet had no doubt become the largest global marketplace.[1]

The document is double-spaced and paragraphs are indented one-half inch.

The commercial potential of the Internet stems from the fact that it is a global network with inexpensive access.[2] The Internet is also available 24x7. The multimedia capability to the Internet is important for marketing and advertising. Quick product delivery, automated order-taking, and low overhead are several more factors that are driving Internet commerce.[3]

A superscript number indicates a footnote or endnote.

Note that the seventh edition of the MLA handbook does not use superscript numbers in the footnote area.

[1] This is the opinion of many business leaders and economists.

[2] This is true in the United States, but some nations still have high rates due to limited competition among Internet service providers.

[3] These factors depend upon the capabilities of individual companies.

TIP You can select the superscripted number in the footnote area and remove the checkmark from the superscript checkbox in the Font dialog box, if necessary.

Working with Footnotes, Endnotes, and Citations

Video Library   http://labyrinthelab.com/videos   Video Number: WD13-V0602

Footnotes, endnotes, and citations are important parts of most research papers. You use them to comment on, or cite a reference to, a designated part of the text. Footnotes appear at the bottom of pages; endnotes, as the name implies, appear at the end of a document or section; and citations appear on a separate Works Cited page at the end of the document. The Works Cited page is another name for a bibliography.

For simplicity, the following topics use the term *footnote* only. All details described for footnotes apply equally to endnotes.

Inserting Footnotes

When you insert a footnote, Word inserts a footnote reference mark in the document and a corresponding mark at the bottom of the page. Word automatically numbers footnotes and renumbers them if you add or delete one. The Footnote and Endnote dialog box offers features for formatting and controlling various aspects of notes.

FROM THE RIBBON
References→Footnotes
→Insert Footnote

FROM THE KEYBOARD
Alt + Ctrl + F to insert a footnote

Indicate if you are dealing with footnotes or endnotes.

Indicate the footnote location: Bottom of Page or Below Text.

You can convert footnotes to endnotes and vice versa.

You can choose a number format or create a custom mark.

You can specify a starting number for each section or page.

Specify if numbering should be continuous or restarted at each section or page.

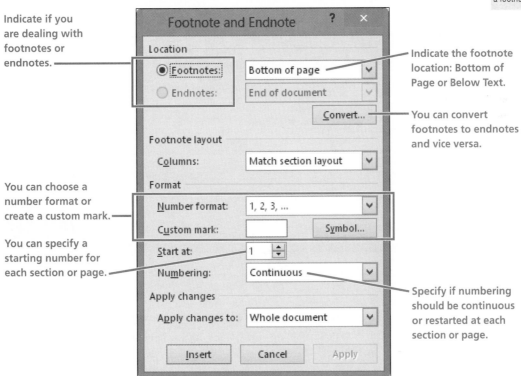

Inserting Citations

You use a citation to refer to material you obtained from an outside source that you are using in the paper. You can enter the source information when you create the citation or insert a placeholder and add the source data later. The citation appears inside parentheses at the end of the cited material; this notation takes the place of the superscript number that is placed for a footnote.

FROM THE RIBBON

References→ Citations & Bibliography→Insert Citation

There are a number of citation systems in addition to the MLA documentation style. Examples include the American Psychological Association (APA) style and the *Chicago Manual of Style* (CMS). The source information relating to the citation appears in a bibliography (or Works Cited page, depending on the citation system), usually at the end of the document. You choose the documentation style when you create the citation. The Create Source dialog box contains different fields depending on the documentation style you select.

Choose the type of source (book, website, etc.).

The source information goes here.

Create Source	? ✕

Type of Source Web site ▾

Bibliography Fields for MLA

Author		Edit
☐ Corporate Author		
Name of Web Page		
Year		
Month		
Day		
Year Accessed		
Month Accessed		
Day Accessed		
Medium		

☐ Show All Bibliography Fields

Tag name

Placeholder1

OK   Cancel

If you need additional fields, check this box.

Word uses tags internally to reference bibliography entries.

Insert Footnotes and Citations

In this exercise, you will create a research paper and insert footnotes and citations, and you will convert footnotes to endnotes.

1. Start **Word**. Open **WD06-D01-Internet** from your **WD2013 Lesson 06** folder and save it as **WD06-D01-Internet-[FirstInitialLastName]**.

   Replace the bracketed text with your first initial and last name. For example, if your name is Bethany Smith, your filename would look like this: WD06-D01-Internet-BSmith.

2. If necessary, choose **View→Views→Print Layout** 📄.

   Footnotes may differ in appearance depending on the view you are using.

3. Position the insertion point at the top of the document and type the four lines of text above the title, tapping Enter once after each line, except the last line.

Simpson-1¶

¶

Brian·Simpson¶

Professor·Williams¶

Marketing·222¶

May·10,·2013¶

Internet·Commerce·and·Its·Effect·on·the·Environment¶

The·Internet·had·its·origins·in·the·1960s·when·the·Department·of·Defense·developed·a·

communications·network·to·connect·the·computers·of·various·military·installations.·The·Department·of·

Notice that the paragraph text is double-spaced and the extra space after the paragraphs has been removed per MLA requirements.

Insert Footnotes

4. Position the insertion point to the right of the period at the end of the first paragraph.

5. Choose **References→Footnotes→Insert Footnote** $\boxed{\text{AB}}^1$.

   Word places the footnote reference mark at the insertion point location, and a corresponding footnote appears at the bottom of the page.

6. Follow these steps to complete the footnote:

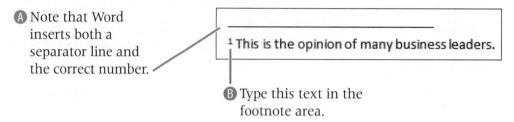

Ⓐ Note that Word inserts both a separator line and the correct number.

Ⓑ Type this text in the footnote area.

¹ This is the opinion of many business leaders.

7. Use the same process to insert the footnote reference marks and associated footnotes shown here.

The commercial potential of the Internet stems from the fact that it is a global network with inexpensive access.² The Internet is also available 24x7. The multimedia capability to the Internet is important for marketing and advertising. Quick product delivery, automated order-taking, and low overhead are several more factors that are driving Internet commerce.³

Internet commerce will be a driving force in the global economy of the twenty-first century. There are still obstacles to overcome, but technology and market forces will propel this new commercial medium forward at a rapid pace.

---

¹ This is the opinion of many business leaders.
² This is true in the United States, but some nations still have high rates due to limited competition among Internet service providers.
³ These factors depend upon the capabilities of individual companies.

The formatting of the footnotes does not adhere to MLA requirements. The text should use the same formatting as the body of the document (double-spaced, first line indented). You will format the footnotes later.

8. Type these paragraphs after the last paragraph.

> The environmental outlook is indeed bright: According to the latest study by Carnegie Mellon University, more than half (about 65%) of total emissions was produced by consumers driving to and from retail stores as opposed to buying online.
>
> Geoffrey Fowler, in his March 3, 2009 article on the Wall Street Journal website cited the following environmental benefits to e-commerce shopping:
>
> - Uses about one-third less energy than conventional retail shopping
> - Uses a one-third smaller carbon footprint than a standard building
> - A truck delivering numerous packages along its way is the largest environmental savings, as it uses less energy per package than if the consumers had driven to the shops themselves.

Convert Footnotes to Endnotes

9. Choose **References→Footnotes→dialog box launcher** ⌄ and click **Convert**.

10. When the Convert Notes box opens, click **OK** and then close the **Footnote and Endnote** dialog box.

11. Scroll through the document and notice that the footnotes are no longer at the bottom of page 1; they now appear as endnotes on the last page.

12. Click **Undo** ↶ to reinstate the footnotes at the bottom of page 1.

Select the MLA Style and Insert a Citation

13. Choose **References→Citations & Bibliography→Style menu** ▼→**MLA Seventh Edition**.

14. Position the insertion point between the word *online* and the period at the end of the first paragraph on page 2; tap [Spacebar].

15. Choose **References→Citations & Bibliography→Insert Citation** ⧉, and then choose **Add New Source**.

16. Follow these steps to create the new source to insert as the citation:

Ⓐ If necessary, choose **Web Site** here.

Ⓑ Type the author's name as shown. Example text appears at the bottom of the window for each field.

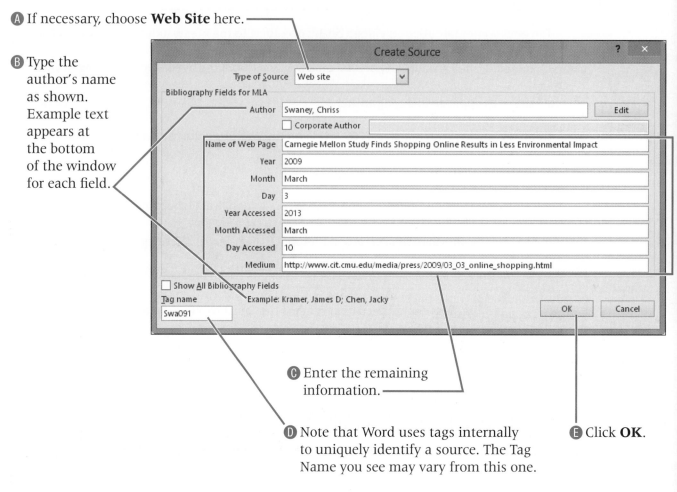

Ⓒ Enter the remaining information.

Ⓓ Note that Word uses tags internally to uniquely identify a source. The Tag Name you see may vary from this one.

Ⓔ Click **OK**.

Notice the author's last name is inserted as the name of the citation.

Remember, Word does not follow all MLA guidelines. Refer to the MLA handbook or website when writing academic papers.

Insert a Citation Placeholder

17. Position the insertion point at the end of the document between *themselves* and the period and tap Spacebar.

18. Choose **Reference→Citations & Bibliography→Insert Citation** ⬇, and then choose **Add New Placeholder**.

19. Follow these steps to create a placeholder for a citation named Fowler:

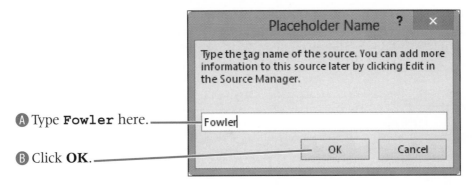

Ⓐ Type **Fowler** here. ——

Ⓑ Click **OK**. ——

20. Save the file.

Editing and Formatting Footnotes

Video Library   http://labyrinthelab.com/videos   Video Number: WD13-V0603

You can edit footnote text directly in the footnote area. In addition to editing the text of a footnote, you can also:

- **Reposition:** You can change the position of a footnote reference mark by dragging it to another location in the document.
- **Format:** You can change various formatting features of footnotes using the Footnote and Endnote dialog box. For example, you can change the numbering scheme, change the starting number, or even replace a footnote number with a special symbol.

In this example, uppercase letters replace the normal numbering for footnotes.

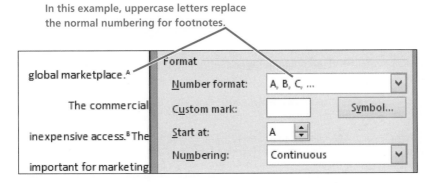

Editing a Footnote

Word's default style for footnote text does not meet MLA documentation style requirements. You must change the formatting if you want to be in compliance with MLA. MLA requirements state the text should be the same formatting as the text in the document; that is, double-spaced with the first line indented. You make those types of formatting changes, as well as editing changes, directly in the footnote area of the document.

Editing a Citation

Once you insert a citation or a citation placeholder you can edit the information in the Edit Source dialog box, which contains the same fields as the Create Source dialog box. The default citation in the body of the document is the author's last name; however, you can choose to suppress it and instead show the name of the web page.

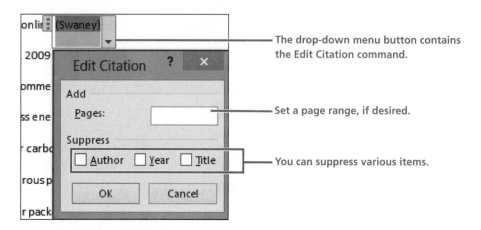

The drop-down menu button contains the Edit Citation command.

Set a page range, if desired.

You can suppress various items.

QUICK REFERENCE	WORKING WITH FOOTNOTES AND CITATIONS
Task	**Procedure**
Insert a footnote	Choose References→Footnotes→Insert Footnote.
Navigate to footnotes	Choose References→Footnotes→Next/Previous Footnote.
Edit/format footnotes in Print Layout view	Edit in the footnote area at the bottom of the page.
Format a footnote	Choose References→Footnotes, click the dialog box launcher, and then make the desired changes.
Delete a footnote	Select the footnote reference mark and tap Delete to delete the reference mark and the note.
Insert a citation	Choose References→Citations & Bibliography→Insert Citation, choose Add New Source, and enter data in the dialog box.
Edit a citation source	Click the citation in the document, click the arrow on the right, choose Edit Source, and make the desired changes.
Edit a citation	Click the citation in the document, click the arrow on the right, choose Edit Citation, and make the desired changes.
Delete a citation	Click the citation in the document, click the handle on the left to select the citation, and tap Delete.

Work with Footnotes and Citations

In this exercise, you will format, edit, and delete footnotes and edit a citation placeholder and source.

1. Save your file as **WD06-D02-Internet-[FirstInitialLastName]**.

2. Position the insertion point at the beginning of the second paragraph on page 1 and scroll, if necessary, to see the three footnote reference marks and the footnotes at the bottom of the page.

3. Choose **References→Footnotes→dialog box launcher** 🖸 to display the Footnote and Endnote dialog box.

4. Follow these steps to change the numbering format:

Ⓐ If necessary, choose **Footnotes.**

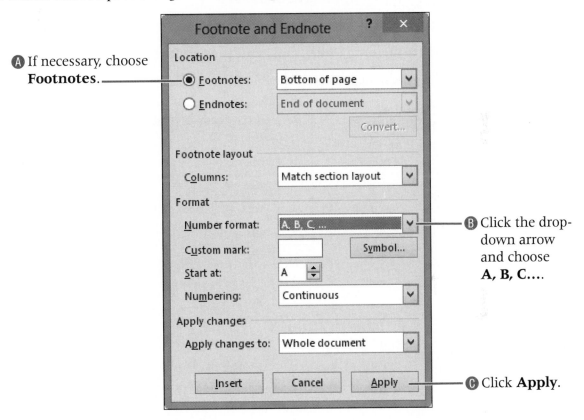

Ⓑ Click the drop-down arrow and choose **A, B, C….**

Ⓒ Click **Apply.**

The footnote numbers change to alphabetic characters. You use the same technique to change the format of endnotes.

5. Click **Undo** 🔄 to return to number formatting.

6. If necessary, choose **View→Show→Ruler** to display the ruler.

7. Select the three footnotes, and then follow these steps to format the footnotes:

   ■ Change line spacing to **double-space**.
   ■ Change the font size to **11 points**.
   ■ On the ruler, drag the **First Line Indent** marker (top triangle) to the **half-inch** mark.

Delete and Edit Footnotes

8. Follow these steps to delete a footnote:

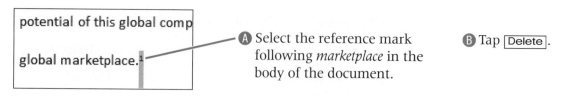

potential of this global comp

global marketplace.[1]

Ⓐ Select the reference mark following *marketplace* in the body of the document.

Ⓑ Tap Delete .

The reference mark and the footnote are removed, and the remaining footnotes renumber.

9. Click **Undo** ↶ to replace the footnote.

10. Position the insertion point between the last word and the period of the first footnote, tap Spacebar , and type **and economists**.

Edit a Citation Placeholder

11. Scroll to the end of page 2 and locate the **Fowler** citation.

12. Follow these steps to open the Edit Source dialog box:

Ⓐ Click the **Fowler** citation placeholder.

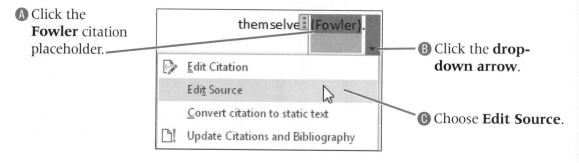

themselve ⁞ (Fowler).

Edit Citation

Edit Source

Convert citation to static text

Update Citations and Bibliography

Ⓑ Click the **drop-down arrow**.

Ⓒ Choose **Edit Source**.

13. Follow these steps to add the source information to the Fowler citation:

Ⓐ If necessary, choose **Web Site**.

Ⓑ Enter the author's name as shown.

Ⓒ Enter the remaining data.

Ⓓ Click **OK**.

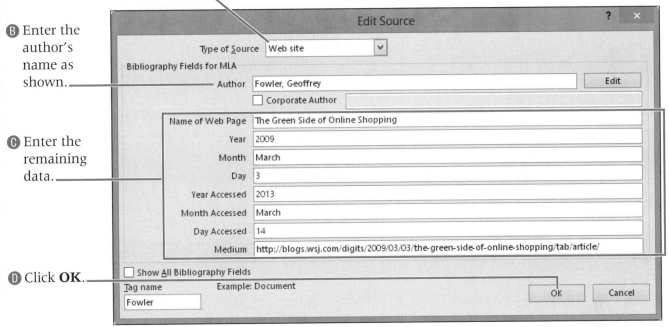

14. Click **Yes** if a message appears asking if you want to update the master list and current document.

The citation may have picked up the name of the web page (title).

15. If necessary, click the drop-down arrow to the right of the Fowler citation and choose **Edit Citation**, check the **Title** box, and click **OK**.

16. Save the file.

Working with Bibliographies

Video Library   http://labyrinthelab.com/videos   Video Number: WD13-V0604

A bibliography is a list of the sources cited in the preparation of the document. Word automatically generates a bibliography based on the source information that you provide in the Create Source dialog box. The bibliography picks up the correct punctuation; however, certain formatting requirements are not Microsoft defaults and must be addressed separately.

The Bibliography button in the Citations & Bibliography group on the References tab contains three built-in options: Bibliography, References, and Works Cited. You can choose any of these; however, the formatting may or may not meet the requirements of the document style you chose. For example, the Works Cited option for the MLA style does not format the title, the paragraph spacing, or the line spacing correctly.

The Bibliography options may not format references as needed. Use the Insert Bibliography command to create citations more precisely.

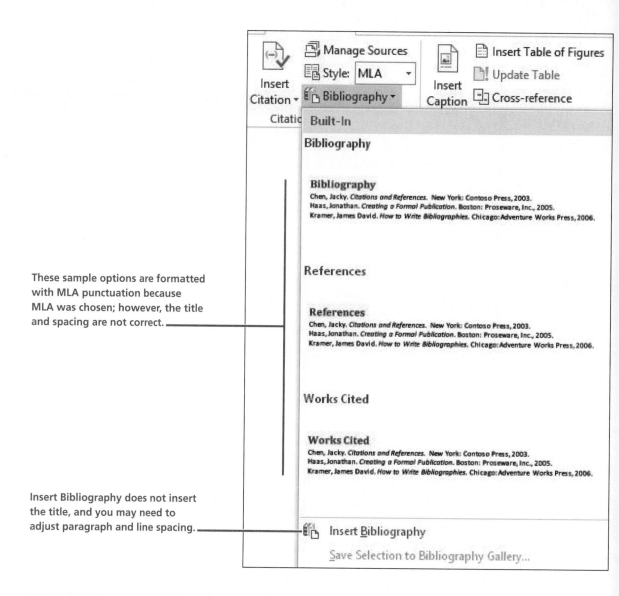

These sample options are formatted with MLA punctuation because MLA was chosen; however, the title and spacing are not correct.

Insert Bibliography does not insert the title, and you may need to adjust paragraph and line spacing.

Updating a Bibliography

When you edit the citation source or add a new one, you can easily update the bibliography list using the Update Field command on the menu when you right-click on the list. The Update Field command reformats the list to single-spacing again; thus, you must remember to change back to double-spacing.

Create a Bibliography

In this exercise, you will create a bibliography for the citations in the document. You will title the page as Works Cited, since the lesson is following the MLA documentation style. Finally, you will edit an existing citation, update the bibliography, and format the paragraphs with double-spacing.

1. Save your file as **WD06-D03-Internet-[FirstInitialLastName]**.

2. Position the insertion point at the end of the document.

3. Tap Enter twice; then, press Ctrl + Enter to insert a new page for the bibliography.

4. Choose **Home→Paragraph→Center** 📄, and then type **Works Cited** and tap Enter.

Insert and Update the Bibliography

5. Choose **References→Citations & Bibliography→Bibliography** 📑.

6. Choose **Insert Bibliography** at the bottom of the menu.

7. Scroll up to the bottom of the second page and click the **Fowler** citation, and then click the arrow on the right.

8. Choose **Edit Source** to open the dialog box.

9. Change the **Day Accessed** to **10** and click **OK**.

10. If the citation picked up the name of the web page, click the drop-down arrow, choose **Edit Citation**, check the **Title** box, and click **OK**.

11. Scroll down the **Works Cited page** and notice nothing has changed yet in the list.

12. Follow these steps to update the bibliography:

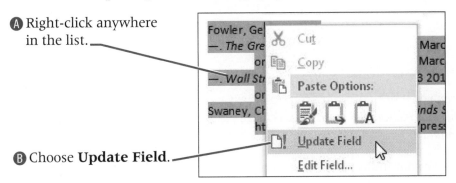

Ⓐ Right-click anywhere in the list.

Ⓑ Choose **Update Field**.

Notice the date accessed for the Fowler citation changed to 10 March 2013.

Format the List

13. Select the bibliography list, but not the Works Cited title.

If you click the list, it highlights in light gray. You must *drag* to select the list, which then highlights in a darker gray.

14. Choose **Home→Paragraph→Line and Paragraph Spacing** 📄, and then choose **2.0**.

15. Save the file.

Inserting Captions and a Table of Figures

Video Library   http://labyrinthelab.com/videos   Video Number: WD13-V0605

You use captions to insert text associated with figures in a paper. Word then uses the captions as entries in the table of figures. Later, if you alter some of the captions, Word updates these when you regenerate the table of figures.

Inserting Captions

Word can automate the creation of captions for certain types of objects. Click AutoCaption and choose the file types you want Word to automatically assign captions to.

The caption text is entered here.

The default label is Figure; Equation and Table are the other options.

Check this box to prevent a word before the number.

You can create a custom label.

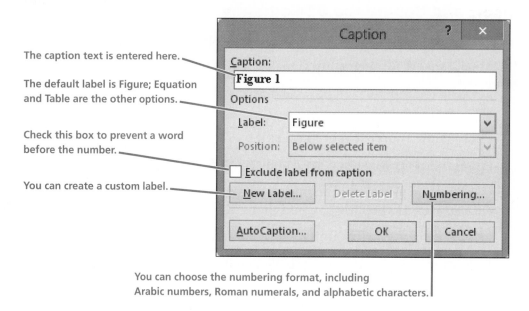

You can choose the numbering format, including Arabic numbers, Roman numerals, and alphabetic characters.

DEVELOP YOUR SKILLS WD06-D04
Add Captions to Figures

In this exercise, you will insert a file between pages 1 and 2 that contains five PowerPoint slides from a presentation. You will add captions to the slides in preparation for creating a table of figures.

1. Save your file as **WD06-D04-Internet-[FirstInitialLastName]**.

2. Position the insertion point after the third footnote reference mark in the body of the document (not the footnote area) at the bottom of the first page.

3. Press `Ctrl` + `Enter` to insert a page break.

4. Choose **Insert→Text→Object** 📑 **menu ▼→Text from File**.

5. In the Insert File dialog box, navigate to your **WD2013 Lesson 06** folder, choose **WD06-D04-Slides**, and click **Insert**.

Add and Edit Captions

6. If necessary, choose **Home→Paragraph→Show/Hide** ¶ to display formatting marks.

7. Position the insertion point on the first blank line below the first slide.

8. Choose **References→Captions→Insert Caption** 🖼.

9. The Caption dialog box should match the following illustration. If *Figure 1* does not appear in the Caption text box, follow these steps. Otherwise, go to step 10.

Ⓐ Click the **Label menu** button and choose **Figure**.

Ⓑ Click **Numbering** to open the **Caption Numbering** dialog box.

Ⓒ Click the **Format menu** button, and then choose the **1, 2, 3, …** format.

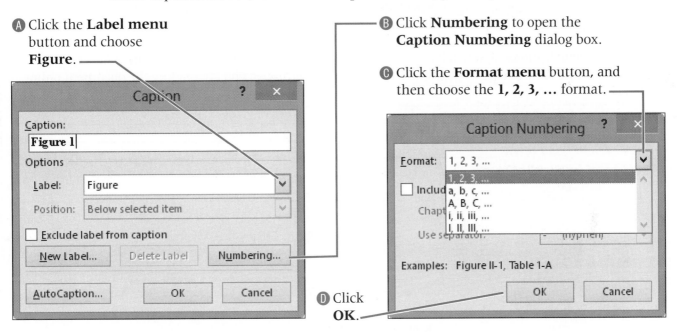

Ⓓ Click **OK**.

10. If necessary, position the insertion point to the right of *Figure 1* in the Caption text box.

11. Tap the ⌨Spacebar, type **DOD and ARPANET**, and click **OK** to insert the caption. *The caption is placed at the left margin.*

12. Choose **Home→Paragraph→Center** ☰.

13. Position the insertion point in the first blank line below the second slide.

14. Choose **References→Captions→Insert Caption** 🖼.

15. Tap the ⌨Spacebar, type **NSF**, and click **OK**.

16. **Center** ☰ the caption.

17. Add these captions and center them:

Slide Number	Caption Text
3	MILNET and TCP/IP
4	First Graphical Browser
5	Netscape

Edit a Caption

18. Return to slide 2, select *NSF*, and type **National Science Foundation** in its place.

19. Save the file.

Inserting a Table of Figures

Video Library   http://labyrinthelab.com/videos   Video Number: WD13-V0606

Academic papers often include a table of figures at the front, which guides the reader to illustrations, charts, tables, and other figures. This is particularly helpful in long documents. The table entries conveniently function as hyperlinks if you are reading the document online.

*Figure 1 DOD and ARPANET*_____ 3
Figure 2 National Science Foundation _____ 3
Figure 3 MILNET and TCP/IP _____ 3
Figure 4 First Graphical Browser _____ 4
*Figure 5 Netscape*_____ 4

QUICK REFERENCE	CREATING CAPTIONS AND TABLES OF FIGURES
Task	**Procedure**
Insert a caption	▪ Choose References→Captions→Insert Caption, and then type the caption text.
Insert a table of figures	▪ Choose References→Captions→Insert Table of Figures, and then make the formatting choices.
Update a table of figures	▪ Right-click the table and choose Update Field.

DEVELOP YOUR SKILLS WD06-D05
Generate a Table of Figures

In this exercise, you will generate a table of figures from the captions you inserted earlier. You will change the numbering format of your captions, and then you will update the table to reflect the change.

Insert the Table of Figures

1. Save your file as **WWD06-D05-Internet-[FirstInitialLastName]**.

2. Move the insertion point to the top of the document and insert a page break.

3. Press Ctrl + Home to position the insertion point at the top of the new page, and then type **Table of Figures** and tap Enter twice.

4. Format the heading you just typed with **center, bold 16 point**.

5. Place the insertion point in the blank line below the heading.

6. Choose **References→Captions→Insert Table of Figures** 📄.

7. Follow these steps to set up the table:

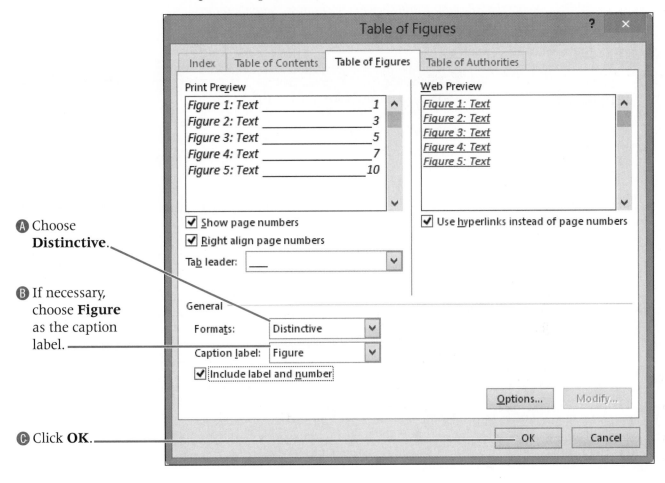

Ⓐ Choose **Distinctive**.

Ⓑ If necessary, choose **Figure** as the caption label.

Ⓒ Click **OK**.

8. Position the insertion point on page 3 so you will be able to see the effect of the next change.

Change the Numbering Format of the Captions

9. Choose **References→Captions→Insert Caption** 📄.

10. Click **Numbering** to display the Caption Numbering dialog box.

11. Choose the **A, B, C, …** format and click **OK**.

12. Click **Close** in the Caption dialog box, and then scroll through the slides.

    Notice that the figure numbers changed to alphabetic characters.

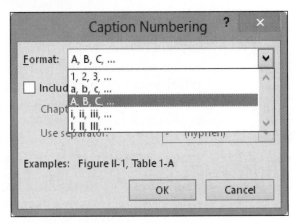

Update the Table of Figures

13. Scroll up to view the **Table of Figures** on page 1.

    Notice that the table is still showing the numeric figure numbers.

14. Follow these steps to update the Table of Figures:

Ⓐ Right-click the table and choose **Update Field**.

Ⓑ Choose this option.

Ⓒ Click **OK**.

| Figure 1 DOD and ARPANET_____ |
| Figure 2 National Science Foundation _ |
| Figure 3 MILNET and TCP/IP _____ |
| Figure 4 First Graphical Browser _____ |
| Figure 5 Netscape _____ |

Update Table of Figures

Word is updating the table of figures. Select one of the following options:

○ Update page numbers only

◉ Update entire table

OK   Cancel

The table should match the following illustration.

Table of Figures

Figure A DOD and ARPANET _____	3
Figure B National Science Foundation _____	3
Figure C MILNET and TCP/IP _____	3
Figure D First Graphical Browser _____	4
Figure E Netscape _____	4

The text switched from Figures 1–5 to Figures A–E.

15. Save and then close the file.

Working with Templates

Video Library   http://labyrinthelab.com/videos   Video Number: WD13-V0607

All Word documents are based on templates, which can include text, formatting, graphics, and any other objects or formats available in Word. The default Word template is Blank Document. The benefit of templates is that they do not change when documents *based on them* change. When you start a new document, Word opens a *copy* of the template. This lets you use templates repeatedly as the basis for new documents. Word provides a variety of ready-to-use templates, or you can also create your own personal templates.

Creating a Document from a Template

Templates are located in the Word Start screen or in Backstage view when you choose the New screen. Basing a new document on a template can save you a lot of time since much of the formatting is already included in the template for you.

If you don't find a template you want in the Featured templates, you can search online by entering your own search term or by choosing a suggested search.

If you create personal templates, click here to view them.

Clicking a template displays a window that describes the template; double-clicking a template immediately opens it in the Word window.

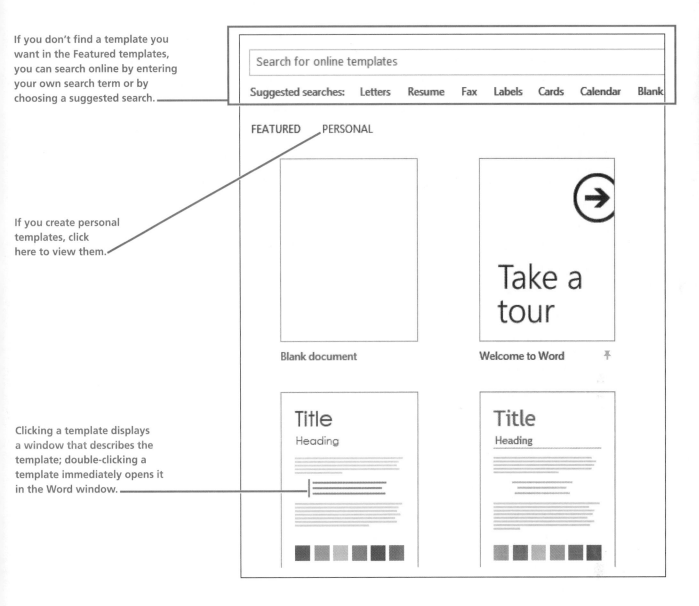

Saving Personal Templates

When you create a document containing specific formatting, you can save it to use later as a template. You should save the template in the Custom Office Templates folder unless instructed to do otherwise. The Custom Office Templates folder is the default in the Save As window when a template is chosen in the Save As Type field. This is what causes your templates to appear when you click the Personal link on the templates screen. You can save a template as a Word Template or as a Word Macro-Enabled Template. A macro-enabled template is one that contains a special series of instructions called a macro.

Choose the template type from the Save As Type list in the Save As window.

Create a Template from an Existing Document

In this exercise, you will open a copy of a report and save it as a template. The body text of the report has been removed; however, other elements are still in place, including the cover page, the table of figures, and the double-spacing. You will then save time by starting a new report based on the template.

1. Open **WD06-D06-MyReport** from your **WD2013 Lesson 06** folder.

2. Scroll through the document and notice the elements that are still in place and that will be useful when you create a new report.

3. Choose **File→Save As**, navigate to any file storage location, and choose **Word Template** from the **Save As Type** list at the bottom of the dialog box.

   Notice the file path that appears at the top of the Save As dialog box. Word defaults to the Custom Office Templates folder in the My Documents folder as the file storage location.

4. Save the file as `WD06-D06-MyReport-[FirstInitialLastName]`.

5. Choose **File→Close** to close the template file.

6. Choose **File→New**.

7. Follow these steps to open a copy of your template:

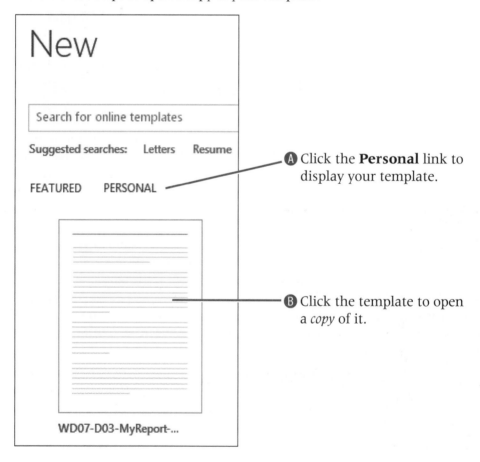

Ⓐ Click the **Personal** link to display your template.

Ⓑ Click the template to open a *copy* of it.

Notice the generic Documentx filename in the title bar at the top of the Word window. This indicates you are working on a copy of the template rather than the template itself.

8. Scroll to page 3 and replace *[DOCUMENT TITLE]* with **Green Life**.

9. Save the document as **WD06-D06-GreenLife-[FirstInitialLastName]** in your **WD2013 Lesson 06** folder.

10. Close the file and exit **Word**.

Deleting a Template

Video Library   http://labyrinthelab.com/videos   Video Number: WD13-V0608

When a template is no longer useful, you may wish to delete it. Templates are easily removed from the Custom Office Templates folder.

QUICK REFERENCE	CREATING AND DELETING TEMPLATES
Task	**Procedure**
Save an existing document as a template	■ Choose File→Save As and navigate to the desired file storage location. ■ Choose Word Template from the Save as Type list, enter the template name, and click Save.
Delete a template	■ Click File Explorer on the taskbar, navigate to the Documents folder, and double-click the Custom Office Templates folder. ■ Choose the desired template and tap Delete.

Delete a Template

In this exercise, you will delete the template you created.

1. Click **File Explorer** 🖿 on the taskbar at the bottom of the screen.

2. Follow these steps to delete the My Report template:

Ⓐ Navigate to the **Documents** folder.

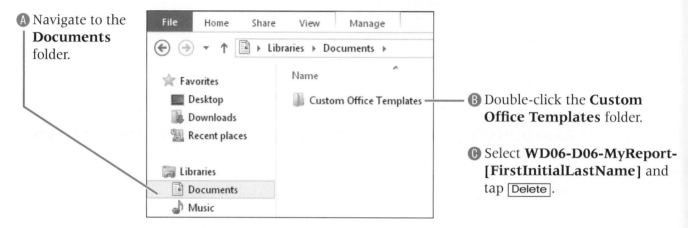

Ⓑ Double-click the **Custom Office Templates** folder.

Ⓒ Select **WD06-D06-MyReport-[FirstInitialLastName]** and tap Delete .

3. Close the **File Explorer** window.

Concepts Review

To check your knowledge of the key concepts introduced in this lesson, complete the Concepts Review quiz by choosing the appropriate access option below.

If you are...	Then access the quiz by...
Using the Labyrinth Video Library	Going to http://labyrinthelab.com/videos
Using eLab	Logging in, choosing Content, and navigating to the Concepts Review quiz for this lesson
Not using the Labyrinth Video Library or eLab	Going to the student resource center for this book

Reinforce Your Skills

Create Footnotes, Endnotes, Citations, and a Bibliography

In this exercise, you will work with endnotes, footnotes, and citations. Then you will generate a bibliography. Although you will select the MLA style in the Citations & Bibliography group, because this research paper is not for academic purposes, you will not follow strict MLA formatting guidelines.

Work with Footnotes and Endnotes

1. Start **Word**. Open **WD06-R01-GlobalLocal** from your **WD2013 Lesson 06** folder and save it as `WD06-R01-GlobalLocal-[FirstInitialLastName]`.

2. Position the insertion point after the period following *sales* in the second paragraph.

> Kids for Change is a non-profit organization that helps minors in their
>
> social/community service within the mindset of "Think Globally, Act Locally."
>
> fundraisers, such as car washes, bake sales, and rain barrel sales. The kids are

3. Choose **References→Footnotes→Insert Endnote** .

4. Type this endnote text.

> ⁱ Proceeds go to organizations, such as the local pantry.

5. Position the insertion point after the comma following *construction* in the second to last line of the second paragraph.

> fundraisers, such as car washes, bake sales, and rain barrel sales.
>
> community recycling drives, researching green construction, and
>
> garden program.

6. Choose **References→Footnotes→Insert Endnote** .

7. Type the endnote text as shown in the following illustration.

> ⅱ Kids for Change successfully encouraged a local businessman to use green construction in a building addition.

You noticed a word is missing in the first endnote, so you will make that change now.

8. In the first endnote, position the insertion point to the left of *pantry*, type **food**, and tap
`Spacebar`.

You've decided to convert the endnotes to footnotes so they will appear on the same page as the text they refer to.

9. Choose **References→Footnotes→dialog box launcher** ⬓.

10. Click **Convert**.

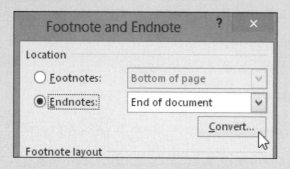

11. When the Convert Notes message appears, click **OK**; close the **Footnote and Endnote** dialog box.

Insert Citations

12. Choose **References→Citations & Bibliography**, and then choose **MLA Seventh Edition** from the Styles drop-down list.

13. Position the insertion point at the end of the fourth bullet point in the **Juniper Russo** citation.

> • Supporting local businesses and agriculture

14. Tap `Spacebar`.

15. Choose **References→Citations & Bibliography→Insert Citation** ⬓, and then choose **Add New Source**.

16. If necessary, choose **Web Site** in the Type of Source drop-down list.

17. Enter the following information in the Create Source dialog box:
    - Author: **Russo, Juniper**
    - Name of Web Page: **What Does "Think Globally, Act Locally" Mean?**
    - Year: **2011**
    - Month: **August**
    - Day: **3**
    - Year Accesses: **2013**
    - Month Accessed: **December**
    - Day Accessed: **15**
    - Medium: **http://voices.yahoo.com/what-does-think-globally-act-locally-mean-8908513.html?cat=57**

18. Click **OK**.

19. Position the insertion point following *Fluids* at the end of the fourth bullet point in the **Jennifer King** citation.

20. Tap Spacebar.

21. Choose **References→Citations & Bibliography→Insert Citation**, and then choose **Add New Source**.

22. Make sure **Web Site** is chosen as the Type of Source.

23. Enter the following information in the Create Source dialog box:
    - Author: **King, Jennifer**
    - Name of Web Page: **How Does Car Pollution Affect the Environment & Ozone Layer?**
    - Year Accessed: **2011**
    - Month Accessed: **December**
    - Day Accessed: **15**
    - Medium: **http://greenliving.nationalgeographic.com/car-pollution-affect-environment-ozone-layer-20133.html**

24. Click **OK**.

25. Position the insertion point at the end of the document between the period and *Nations*.

26. Tap Spacebar.

27. Choose **References→Citations & Bibliography→Insert Citation**, and then choose **Add New Source**.

28. Make sure **Web Site** is chosen as the Type of Source.

29. Enter the following information in the Create Source dialog box:
   - Author: **Trex, Ethan**
   - Name of Web Page: **Whatever Happened to the Hole in the Ozone Layer?**
   - Year: **2012**
   - Month: **May**
   - Day: **23**
   - Year Accessed: **2013**
   - Month Accessed: **December**
   - Day Accessed: **15**
   - Medium: **http://www.mentalfloss.com/blogs/archives/127568**

30. Click **OK**.

Generate and Update a Bibliography

31. Position the insertion point at the end of the document, tap `Enter` twice, and press `Ctrl` + `Enter` to insert a new page for the bibliography.

32. Choose **Home→Paragraph→Center** 📄, type **Works Cited**, and tap `Enter`.

33. Choose **References→Citations & Bibliography→Bibliography** 📄.

34. Choose **Insert Bibliography** at the bottom of the menu.
   Now you'll make a change to a citation.

35. Scroll to and click the **King** citation at the bottom of page 1.

36. Click the arrow on the right and choose **Edit Source**.

37. Change the **Year Accessed** to **2013** and click **OK**.

38. If you are prompted to update the master list, click **Yes**.

39. Scroll to the **Works Cited** page, right-click the list, and choose **Update Field**.
   The year accessed changes to 2013.

40. Save and close the file; exit from **Word**.

41. Submit your final file based on the guidelines provided by your instructor.
   To view examples of how your file or files should look at the end of this exercise, go to the student resource center.

Insert Captions and a Table of Figures, and Create a Template

In this exercise, you will add captions to figures and create a table of figures. Then you will create a letter template.

Insert Captions

1. Start **Word**. Open **WD06-R02-Sustainable** from your **WD2013 Lesson 06** folder and save it as `WD06-R02-Sustainable-[FirstInitialLastName]`.

2. If necessary, choose **Home→Paragraph→Show/Hide ¶** to turn on formatting marks.

3. Position the insertion point on the first blank line following the **Healthy, Safe Home** slide.

4. Choose **References→Captions→Insert Caption**.

5. If necessary, change the Label field to **Figure**, click the Numbering button, and change the format to **1, 2, 3, …**; click **OK**.

6. Choose **Home→Paragraph→Center**.

7. Tap Spacebar and type **Healthy, Safe Home**.

8. Use the same procedure to type the following captions for the remaining slides:
   - **Transportation**
   - **Reduce and Reuse**
   - **Recycle**

Insert a Table of Figures

9. Position the insertion point at the top of the document and press Ctrl + Enter to insert a page break.

10. Press Ctrl + Home to position the insertion point at the top of the document.

11. Type **Table of Figures** and tap Enter twice.

12. **Center** the heading you just typed, and then position the insertion point on the blank line below the heading.

13. Choose **References→Captions→Insert Table of Figures**.

14. If necessary, choose **Formal** as the format and make sure the caption label is **Figure**; click **OK**.

15. Save and then close the file.

Create a Template from an Existing Document

16. Open **WD06-R02-Letter** from your **WD2013 Lesson 06** folder.

    Notice that the letter is already set up with placeholders for the variables.

17. Choose **File→Save As**, navigate to any file storage location, and choose **Word Template** from the Save As Type list.

    The Custom Office Templates folder appears at the top of the Save As dialog box.

18. Save the file as WD06-R02-Letter-[FirstInitialLastName].

19. Choose **File→Close** to close the **Template file**.

20. Choose **File→New**, and then click the **Personal** link toward the top of the New screen.

21. Click your template thumbnail to open a copy of it.

22. Enter the current date, and then replace the inside address and greeting placeholders with information of your choice.

23. Save the file as WD06-R02-FormLtr-[FirstInitialLastName] in the **WD2013 Lesson 06** folder; close the file.

Delete a Template

24. Click **File Explorer** ▨ on the taskbar at the bottom of the screen.

25. Navigate to the **Documents folder** in the left panel.

26. Double-click the **Custom Office Templates** folder on the right.

27. Select **WD06-R02-Letter-[FirstInitialLastName]** and tap ⌷Delete⌷.

28. Close **File Explorer**, and then, if necessary, exit from **Word**.

29. Submit your final file based on the guidelines provided by your instructor.

    To view examples of how your file or files should look at the end of this exercise, go to the student resource center.

REINFORCE YOUR SKILLS WD06-R03

Format and Distribute a Research Paper

In this exercise, you will insert a footnote and citations in an organic food research paper. You will choose the MLA style; however, since this is not an academic paper, you will not follow strict MLA formatting guidelines. Then you will insert captions, generate a table of figures, and create a template.

Work with Footnotes and Citations

1. Start **Word**. Open **WD06-R03-OrganicFood** from your **WD2013 Lesson 06** folder, and save it as WD06-R03-OrganicFood-[FirstInitialLastName].

2. If necessary, choose **Home→Paragraph→Show/Hide** ¶ to turn on formatting marks.

3. Position the insertion point to the right of the period at the end of the first paragraph.

4. Choose **References→Footnotes→Insert Footnote** AB[1].

5. Type this text in the footnote area.

---

[1] See Sustainable Animal Agriculture for details on raising animals with care.

Now you will choose the style for citations.

6. Choose **Reference→Citations & Bibliography**, click the **Style menu button** ▾, and choose **MLA Seventh Edition**.

7. Position the insertion point between the period and the word *bay* at the end of the second paragraph below the *Plant Production* heading, and tap ⌐Spacebar¬.

8. Choose **References→Citations & Bibliography→Insert Citation** 🗎, and then choose **Add New Source**.

9. Make sure **Web Site** is chosen as the Type of Source.

10. Enter the following information:
    - Author: `Mayo Clinic, Staff`
    - Name of Web Page: `Nutrition and healthy eating`
    - Year Accessed: `2013`
    - Month Accessed: `December`
    - Day Accessed: `15`
    - Medium: `http://www.mayoclinic.com/health/organic-food/NU00255`

11. Click **OK**.

    The citation may have picked up the name of the web page (title).

12. If necessary, click the drop-down arrow to the right of the citation and choose **Edit Citation**, check the **Title** box, and click **OK**.

13. Position the insertion point at the end of the fourth bullet point below the *Benefits of Organic Food* heading and tap ⌐Spacebar¬.

14. Choose **References→Citations & Bibliography→Insert Citation** 🗎, and then choose **Add New Source**.

15. Ensure that **Web Site** is the Type of Source.

16. Enter the following information:
    - Author: `Blake, Daniel`
    - Name of Web Page: `13 Benefits of Organic Food`
    - Year: `2012`
    - Month: `December`
    - Day: `10`
    - Year Accessed: `2013`
    - Month Accessed: `December`
    - Day Accessed: `13`
    - Medium: `http://ecoscraps.com/13-benefits-organic-food/`

17. Click **OK**.

Work with a Bibliography

18. Position the insertion point at the end of the document and press [Ctrl]+[Enter] to insert a page break.

19. Choose **Home→Paragraph→Center** ☰, and then type `Works Cited` and tap [Enter].

20. Choose **References→Citations & Bibliography→Bibliography** 🗐, and then choose **Insert Bibliography** at the bottom of the menu.

    Next you will edit the footnote and a citation, and update the bibliography.

21. Click the **Blake** citation on page one, click the arrow, and choose **Edit Source**.

22. Change the Month Accessed to `November` and click **OK**.

23. Click **Yes** if you are prompted to update both lists.

24. Scroll to the bibliography, right-click the list, and choose **Update Field**.

    The month accessed changes to November.

Inserting Captions and a Table of Figures

25. Position the insertion point on the first blank line below the first picture.

26. Choose **References→Captions→Insert Caption** 🖼.

27. If necessary, choose **Figure** in the Label field and make sure the numbering format is **1, 2, 3, …**.

28. If necessary, position the insertion point to the right of **Figure 1** in the Caption text box.

29. Tap [Spacebar], type `Better for the Soil`, and click **OK**.

30. Position the insertion point in the first blank line below the second picture.

31. Choose **References→Captions→Insert Caption** 🖼.

32. Tap [Spacebar], type `Better for the Water`, and click **OK**.

33. Follow the same process to place a caption titled `Increases Consumer Choices` below the third picture and `Fresher, Better Tasting` below the fourth picture.

34. Press [Ctrl]+[Home] to position the insertion point at the top of the document.

35. Press [Ctrl]+[Enter] to insert a page break; position the insertion point at the top of the first page.

36. Type `Table of Figures` and tap [Enter] twice.

37. Select the heading and apply **center, bold 16 points** formatting.

38. Position the insertion point on the blank line below the heading.

39. Choose **References→Captions→Insert Table of Figures** 🗐.

40. In the dialog box, choose **Distinctive** as the format style, ensure that the caption label is **Figure**, and click **OK**.

    Now you'll change the number format style for the captions and update the Table of Figures.

41. Choose **References→Captions→Insert Caption** 🖼→**Numbering**.

42. Choose the **i, ii, iii, …** format and click **OK**.

43. Close the **Caption** dialog box, and then scroll through the pictures and notice the change to lowercase Roman numerals.

44. Scroll to the **Table of Figures** on page 1, right-click the table, and choose **Update Field**.

45. If necessary, choose **Update Entire Table** and click **OK**.

    Notice the figure numbers updated in the table.

46. Save and then close the file.

Create and Delete a Template

Kids for Change will use this document as a handout when giving organic food presentations at community schools. They will send a letter, along with the document, to the school principals for their approval. They will create a template they can use repeatedly for this task.

47. Open the **WD06-R03-PrincipalLtr** from your **WD2013 Lesson 06** folder.

48. Choose **File→Save As**, navigate to any file storage location, and choose **Word Template** from the Save As Type list.

    Notice that Word switches to the Custom Office Templates folder as the file storage location.

49. Save the file as `WD06-R03-PrincipalLtr-[FirstInitialLastName]`, and then choose **File→Close** to close the template file.

    Now you'll open a copy of the template.

50. Choose **File→New**, and then click the **Personal** link to display your template.

51. Click the template thumbnail to open a copy of the template.

52. Save the file as `WD06-R03-PrinLtrFinal-[FirstInitialLastName]` in the **WD2013 Lesson 06** folder.

53. Delete the placeholder text for the date; enter the current date.

54. Replace the placeholder text for the inside address with the following inside address:

    ```
    Ms. Eleanor Roberts
    Bascom High School
    951 Elm Street
    Annapolis, MD 21405
    ```

55. Replace the salutation placeholder name with `Ms. Roberts`.

56. Replace the member name with your name.

57. Save and then close the file.

    Now you will delete the template.

58. Click **File Explorer** 🗔 on the taskbar at the bottom of the screen.

59. Navigate to the **Documents** folder in the left-hand panel.

60. Double-click the **Custom Office Templates** folder on the right.

61. Select the **WD06-R03-PrincipalLtr-[FirstInitialLastName]** file and tap `Delete`.

62. Close **File Explorer**; exit from **Word**.

63. Submit your final files based on the guidelines provided by your instructor.

Apply Your Skills

Work with Footnotes, Citations, and a Bibliography

In this exercise, you will create a report detailing some Italian tourist sites and providing tips on train travel in Italy. You will insert footnotes and citations, generate a bibliography, edit a citation, and update the bibliography. Since this is not an academic report, you will not hold to strict MLA guidelines.

Insert Footnotes

1. Start **Word**. Open **WD06-A01-Italy** from your **WD2013 Lesson 06** folder and save it as `WD06-A01-Italy-[FirstInitialLastName]`.

2. Position the insertion point at the end of the first paragraph in the document.

3. Insert this footnote: `Other major attractions are listed on this website.`

4. Position the insertion point after the period following the word *choices* in the paragraph beginning, *In the article, "Italy Train Travel….*

5. Insert this footnote: `This article also offers advice on train schedules, buying tickets, and boarding your train.`

Enter Citations and Create a Bibliography

6. Choose **MLA Seventh Edition** as the style in the Citations & Bibliography group on the References tab.

7. Position the insertion point after the **Colosseum** bullet point near the top of the document.

8. Tap ⎡Spacebar⎤, ensure that **Web Site** is the Type of Source, and enter the following citation information:
   - Author: `Rome Travel, Guide`
   - Name of Web Page: `Rome travel guide`
   - Year Accessed: `2013`
   - Month Accessed: `May`
   - Day Accessed: `23`
   - Medium: `http://www.rome.info/`

9. Click **OK**.

10. Position the insertion point after *Trastevere* at the end of the third bullet point below the *Off the Beaten Path* heading.

11. Tap ⌷Spacebar⌷, ensure that **Web Site** is the Type of Source, and enter the following information:
    - Author: **Casura, Lily**
    - Name of Web Page: **Rome off the beaten path**
    - Year Accessed: **2013**
    - Month Accessed: **May**
    - Day Accessed: **23**
    - Medium: **http://www.tripadvisor.com/Guide-g187791-1295-Rome_ Lazio.html**

12. Click **OK**.

13. Position the insertion point between *more* and the period at the end of the last paragraph.

14. Tap ⌷Spacebar⌷, ensure that **Web Site** is the Type of Source, and enter the following information:
    - Author: **Bakerjian, Martha**
    - Name of Web Page: **Italy Train Travel – Tips on Riding Italian Trains**
    - Year Accessed: **2013**
    - Month Accessed: **May**
    - Day Accessed: **23**
    - Medium: **http://goitaly.about.com/od/italytransportation/a/ trains.htm**

15. Click **OK**.

16. Position the insertion point at the end of the document, tap ⌷Enter⌷ twice, and insert a page break.

17. Type **Works Cited** as the heading and tap ⌷Enter⌷.

18. **Center** ☰ the heading; position the insertion point on the blank line below the heading.

19. Insert a bibliography on the new page using the **Insert Bibliography** command.
    Now you will edit a citation and then update the bibliography.

20. Edit the **Casura** citation source on page 1 by changing the month accessed to **September**. If you are prompted to update the source, click Yes.

21. Update the bibliography and check that the change to the Casura citation is there.

22. Save and then close the file; exit from **Word**.

23. Submit your final file based on the guidelines provided by your instructor.
    To view examples of how your file or files should look at the end of this exercise, go to the student resource center.

Insert Captions and a Table of Figures, and Create a Template

One of Universal Corporate Events' clients plans to send their high sales achievers on an African safari as a reward for their hard work. They are preparing a handout to use in conjunction with their presentation. In this exercise, you will add captions to pictures and generate a table of figures. Then you will create a template from an existing letter.

Insert Captions and Create a Table of Figures

1. Start **Word**. Open **WD06-A02-Safari** from your **WD2013 Lesson 06** folder and save it as `WD06-A02-Safari-[FirstInitialLastName]`.

2. Insert and **center** ☰ the following captions for the pictures in your Safari document; use the **1, 2, 3, …** number format and the **Figure** label.
   - Picture 1 caption: `Wildebeest`
   - Picture 2 caption: `Elephants`
   - Picture 3 caption: `Rhinos`
   - Picture 4 caption: `Leopard`
   - Picture 5 caption: `Lion`
   - Picture 6 caption: `Buffalo`

3. Position the insertion point at the top of the document and insert a page break.

4. Position the insertion point at the top of the new page, type **Table of Figures**, and tap ⌤Enter twice.

5. Format your heading with **center, bold 16 points**.

6. Position the insertion point on the blank line below the heading and generate the table of figures using the **Distinctive** format and **Figure** as the caption label.
   Next you will edit two captions and then regenerate the table of figures.

7. The Leopard and Lion captions should be plural, so add an **s** to the end of each of the captions.

8. Update the entire table of figures and check to make sure the changes took place.

9. Save and then close the file.

Work with a Template

Universal Corporate Events needs to send travel information to the people going on safari, so they will create a template letter that they can use for all the participants.

10. Open **WD06-A02-SafariLtr** from your **WD2013 Lesson 06** folder.
    Notice the variables in uppercase.

11. Save the file as a **Word Template** in the default **Custom Office Templates** folder; choose **File→Close** to close the template.

12. Choose **File→New** and access your **personal templates**.

13. Open a copy of the template, replace the variable text with the current date, inside address, and salutation of your choice. Enter you own name as the travel agent.

14. Save the file as **WD06-A02-SafariLtrFinal-[FirstInitialLastName]** in your **WD2013 Lesson 06** folder; close the file and exit from **Word**.

    Now you will delete the template.

15. Open **File Explorer** from the taskbar, navigate to the **Documents** folder, open the **Custom Office Templates** folder, and delete your template.

16. Close **File Explorer**.

17. Submit your final files based on the guidelines provided by your instructor.

    To view examples of how your file or files should look at the end of this exercise, go to the student resource center.

APPLY YOUR SKILLS WD06-A03

Work with Footnotes, Citations, Captions, and Templates

The intern at Universal Corporate Events has been asked to research travel in Thailand for one of the corporate clients. In this exercise, you will use some of your report-writing skills to help her create her report. Since this is not academic research, you will not conform to strict MLA guidelines.

Work with Footnotes

1. Start **Word**. Open **WD06-A03-Bangkok** from your **WD2013 Lesson 06** folder and save it as **WD06-A03-Bangkok-[FirstInitialLastName]**.

2. Position the insertion point to the right of *markets* in the first line and insert this footnote.

   ---
   [1] Floating markets piled high with tropical fruits and vegetables provide an easy day trip from Bangkok.

3. Position the insertion point to the right of *temples* in the first line and insert this footnote.

   [2] Don't miss Wat Traimit's Golden Buddha or Wat Pho's famous Reclining Buddha.

   Now you will edit the second footnote.

4. Insert the word **renowned** before *Golden*.

Use Citations and Generate a Bibliography

5. Choose the **MLA Seventh Edition** style for citations.

   Now you will insert a citation at the end of the first bullet point.

6. Ensure that **Web Site** is the Type of Source and enter the following information:
   - Author: **Thyberg, David**
   - Name of Web Page: **Bangkok Travel Tips**
   - Year Accessed: **2013**
   - Month Accessed: **September**
   - Day Accessed: **22**
   - Medium: **http://getawaytips.azcentral.com/bangkok-travel-tips-1945.html**

   Now you will insert a citation at the end of the last bullet point on page 1.

7. Ensure that **Web Site** is the Type of Source and enter the following information:
   - Author: **Doman, Gaby**
   - Name of Web Page: **Off the Beaten Track**
   - Year Accessed: **2013**
   - Month Accessed: **September**
   - Day Accessed: **22**
   - Medium: **http://www.tripadvisor.com/Guide-g293916-1104-Bangkok.html**

   Next you will insert a citation at the end of the last bullet point on page 2.

8. Ensure that **Web Site** is the Type of Source and enter the following information:
   - Author: **Rowthorn, Chris**
   - Name of Web Page: **Take the boat out of Bangkok**
   - Year: **2012**
   - Month: **April**
   - Day: **13**
   - Year Accessed: **2013**
   - Month Accessed: **September**
   - Day Accessed: **22**
   - Medium: **http://www.lonelyplanet.com/thailand/bangkok/travel-tips-and-articles/77110**

9. Add a new page at the end of the document for the bibliography, title the page **Works Cited**, and tap Enter .

10. **Center** ≣ the heading; generate the bibliography on a blank line below the title using the **Insert Bibliography** command.

   Now you'll modify a citation and regenerate the bibliography.

11. Change the date accessed for the **Doman** citation to **August 27**.

12. If a message appears asking if you want to update both lists, click **Yes**.

13. Regenerate the bibliography and check that the change was made.

14. Save and close the **Bangkok** file.

Insert Captions and Create a Table of Figures

The Universal Corporate Events art department has created several logo images for the company to use in its pre-travel seminar announcements. The head of the department is asking for input from the stakeholders.

15. Open **WD06-A03-Logo** from your **WD2013 Lesson 06** folder and save it as `WD06-A03-Logo-[FirstInitialLastName]`.

16. If necessary, display formatting marks.

17. Position the insertion point on the first blank line below the first logo image.

18. Open the **Caption dialog box** and ensure that the label is **Figure** and the numbering choice is **1, 2, 3, ...**.

19. Enter and **Center** ▤ the following captions for all of the logos in the order indicated here.
    - Picture 1 caption: `Option 1`
    - Picture 2 caption: `Option 2`
    - Picture 3 caption: `Option 3`
    - Picture 4 caption: `Option 4`
    - Picture 5 caption: `Option 5`

20. Position the insertion point at the end of the document and insert a **page break**.

21. Type `Table of Figures` at the top of the new page and tap [Enter].

22. If necessary, **center** ▤ the heading; apply **bold** B.

23. Generate the table on the blank line below the heading using the **Formal** format and **Figure** as the caption label.

24. Save and close the file.

Create a Template

Universal Corporate Events wants to standardize the branding for their pre-travel seminar announcements and save it as a template they can use repeatedly.

25. Open **WD06-A03-Seminar** from your **WD2013 Lesson 06** folder.

    Notice the elements of the announcement that will work for any travel seminar.

26. Save the file as a template in the **Custom Office Templates** folder, naming it `WD06-A03-Seminar-[FirstInitialLastName]`.

27. Close the template.

28. Open a copy of the template and replace the *[DESTINATION]* placeholder with `Central America`.

29. Save the file as `WD06-A03-SeminarFinal-[FirstInitialLastName]` in your **WD2013 Lesson 06** folder; close the file.

    Next you will delete the template.

30. Open **File Explorer**; navigate to the **Documents** folder and then to the **Custom Office Template** folder.

31. Delete **WD06-A03-Seminar-[FirstInitialLastName]**.

32. Close **File Explorer**; if necessary, exit from **Word**.

33. Submit your final files based on the guidelines provided by your instructor.

Extend Your Skills

In the course of working through the Extend Your Skills exercises, you will think critically as you use the skills taught in the lesson to complete the assigned projects. To evaluate your mastery and completion of the exercises, your instructor may use a rubric, with which more points are allotted according to performance characteristics. (The more you do, the more you earn!) Ask your instructor how your work will be evaluated.

WD06-E01 That's the Way I See It

You are an intern working for a major grocery store chain. Your manager has asked you to research the pros and cons of reusable shopping bags compared to plastic bags. You have decided to follow MLA conventions in your research paper. Start a new Word document named **WD06-E01-ShopBags-[FirstInitialLastName]** and saved to your **WD2013 Lesson 06** folder.

Type an original introductory paragraph for the paper, and include two footnote comments in the paragraph.

Using the search engine of your choice, find two sources who favor reusable shopping bags and two sources who do not. Pull information from these sources into your research paper, compare the two sides of the issue, and present your opinion. Insert citations at the end of each source and generate a bibliography for the citations.

Open **WD06-E01-ShopBags** from your **WD2013 Lesson 06** folder. Copy and paste the pictures into your research paper, add creative captions to the figures, and create a table of figures.

You will be evaluated based on the inclusion of all elements specified, your ability to follow directions, your ability to apply newly learned skills to a real-world situation, your creativity, and the relevance of your topic and/or data choice(s). Submit your final file based on the guidelines provided by your instructor.

WD06-E02 Be Your Own Boss

As the owner of Blue Jean Landscaping, you plan to hold a rose-pruning seminar for your customers. You will research correct pruning techniques and create a report of your research results to hand out to customers at the event. Write an original introductory paragraph of at least five sentences, and cite three different sources in your report using the MLA Seventh Edition style. Then generate a bibliography of your citations. Because this is not an academic paper, you will not follow strict MLA guidelines. Save your file as **WD06-E02-RoseSeminar-[FirstInitialLastName]** in your **WD2013 Lesson 06** folder.

Create a letter template with variable placeholders that will be used to notify customers of the seminar. Save the template as **WD06-E02-Template-[FirstInitialLastName]**. Use a copy of the template to generate a sample customer letter named **WD06-E02-SampleLetter-[FirstInitialLastName]**. Store the files in your **WD2013 Lesson 06** folder.

You will be evaluated based on the inclusion of all elements specified, your ability to follow directions, your ability to apply newly learned skills to a real-world situation, your creativity, and your demonstration of an entrepreneurial spirit. Submit your final files based on the guidelines provided by your instructor.

Transfer Your Skills

In the course of working through the Transfer Your Skills exercises, you will use critical-thinking and creativity skills to complete the assigned projects using skills taught in the lesson. To evaluate your mastery and completion of the exercises, your instructor may use a rubric, with which more points are allotted according to performance characteristics. (The more you do, the more you earn!) Ask your instructor how your work will be evaluated.

WD06-T01 WebQuest: Use the Web as a Learning Tool

Throughout this book, you will be provided with an opportunity to use the Internet as a learning tool by completing WebQuests. According to the original creators of WebQuests, as described on their website (WebQuest.org), a WebQuest is "an inquiry-oriented activity in which most or all of the information used by learners is drawn from the web." To complete the WebQuest projects in this book, navigate to the student resource center and choose the WebQuest for the lesson on which you are currently working. The subject of each WebQuest will be relevant to the material found in the lesson.

WebQuest Subject: Elements of a research paper based on the MLA Seventh Edition documentation style.

Submit your final file(s) based on the guidelines provided by your instructor.

WD06-T02 Demonstrate Proficiency

The owner of Stormy BBQ is proud to use free-range cattle. He wants his employees to understand the benefits of using natural, grass-fed beef so they can discuss the idea with customers. He has asked you to prepare a report that he can distribute to all employees. Start a new Word document named **WD06-T02-GrassFed-[FirstInitialLastName]** and saved to your **WD2013 Lesson 06** folder. Conduct online research on the benefits of using free-range, natural beef. Write an original introductory paragraph of at least five sentences that includes two commentary footnotes. Cite three sources who favor free-range beef. Generate a bibliography for the citations using the MLA Seventh Edition style, but because this is not an academic paper, you don't need to follow strict MLA guidelines.

Open **WD06-T02-Cattle** from your **WD2013 Lesson 06** folder. Copy and paste the pictures into your report, insert creative captions for the pictures, and generate a table of figures.

Submit your final file based on the guidelines provided by your instructor.

WORD 2013

Using Mail Merge

LEARNING OBJECTIVES

After studying this lesson, you will be able to:

- Work with data sources
- Create main documents
- Perform a mail merge
- Work with merge problems
- Generate envelopes and labels

In this lesson, you will manage mail using Word 2013's Mail Merge feature. You will set up data sources where you store name and address information, and you will set up form letters. Then you'll merge your form letters with a data source to produce personalized letters. You'll also generate personalized envelopes and labels. Because you only type the main document once, you only have to proof it once—versus proofing many individually typed letters. When you've validated a data source, you can use it repeatedly without having to check the variable information each time.

Generating a Marketing Mass Mailing

You are the administrative assistant for Green Clean. The company wants to expand their business, and the marketing manager has chosen mass mailings as a good way to generate new prospects. You have been tasked with creating the mailing for the upcoming sales campaign. Mail Merge will save you many hours that would have otherwise been spent addressing each letter individually.

719 Coronado Drive
San Diego, California 92102

Today's Date

Mr. Andre Adams
Mills Insurance
2224 Culver Drive
San Diego, CA 92102

Dear Andre:

Green Clean is a locally owned and operated commercial janitorial service. Our employees are highly trained, and our supervisors check on every job every night to ensure the best quality work.

We follow all EPA guidelines and comply with OSHA standards. We use only environmentally safe cleaning products, providing you with a healthy, nontoxic, clean place of business.

Good customer service is our number one priority. Our proactive account managers stay in touch with our clients and follow through on all requests. We have been in business over twenty years and we have scores of long-term clients.

Andre, one of our account managers will contact you in the near future to discuss you janitorial needs.

Sincerely,

Ahn Tran
President

Variable codes in the form letter merge with the data source to generate personalized letters.

Introducing Mail Merge

Video Library   http://labyrinthelab.com/videos   Video Number: WD13-V0701

Word's Mail Merge feature is most often used for generating personalized form letters, mailing labels, and envelopes. However, Mail Merge is a versatile tool that can be used with any type of document that combines boilerplate text with variable information, such as standard contracts and legal verbiage. Mail Merge can be a big time-saver and is valuable for managing large mailings.

Components of Mail Merge

Merging creates a merged document by combining information from two files. They are known as the main document and the data source.

- **Main document:** This document controls the merge. It contains the fixed information into which the variable information is merged. A typical form letter, for instance, has a different inside address and greeting line in each letter, while the rest of the text is the same for everyone receiving the letter.
- **Data source:** The data source can be another Word document, a spreadsheet, a database file, or a contacts list in Outlook.
- **Merged document:** This document is the result of the merge. It contains all of the letters addressed to each individual in your data source.

You can merge an existing main document with an existing data source, or you can create the main document and data source while stepping through the merge process.

719 Coronado Drive
San Diego, California 92102

Today's Date

«AddressBlock»

«GreetingLine»

Green Clean is a locally owned and operated commercial janitorial service. Our employees are highly trained, and our supervisors check on every job every night to ensure the best quality work.

We follow all EPA guidelines and comply with OSHA standards. We use only environmentally safe cleaning products, providing you with a healthy, nontoxic, clean place of business.

Good customer service is our number one priority. Our proactive account managers stay in touch with our clients and follow through on all requests. We have been in business over twenty years and we have scores of long-term clients.

«First_Name», one of our account managers will contact you in the near future to discuss you janitorial needs.

Sincerely,

Ahn Tran
President

Last N...	First...	Title	Company Name	Address Line 1	City	State	ZIP Code
Adams	Andre	Mr.	Mills Insurance	2224 Culver Drive	San Diego	CA	92102
Bouras	Talos	Mr.	Conrad Corporation	854 Whitmore Drive	San Diego	CA	92101
Chowdery	Michael	Mr.	Seligman Enterprises	146 Meadow Lane	La Jolla	CA	92103
Novarro	Derek	Mr.	Gourmet Warehouse	3300 Maple Drive	La Jolla	CA	92103
Romero	Nicole	Ms.	Harris Health Services	132 Lake Street	San Diego	CA	92101
Wright	Mary	Ms.	Rogers Electric Company	1240 Potrero Avenue	San Diego	CA	92101

The data source can be a Mail Merge recipient list, a Word table, an Excel database, or an Access table.

The main document contains standard text and merge codes where variables from the data source will be merged.

719 Coronado Drive
San Diego, California 92102

Today's Date

Mr. Andre Adams
Mills Insurance
2224 Culver Drive
San Diego, CA 92102

Dear Andre:

Green Clean is a locally owned and operated commercial janitorial service. Our employees are highly trained, and our supervisors check on every job every night to ensure the best quality work.

We follow all EPA guidelines and comply with OSHA standards. We use only environmentally safe cleaning products, providing you with a healthy, nontoxic, clean place of business.

Good customer service is our number one priority. Our proactive account managers stay in touch with our clients and follow through on all requests. We have been in business over twenty years and we have scores of long-term clients.

Andre, one of our account managers will contact you in the near future to discuss you janitorial needs.

Sincerely,

Ahn Tran
President

The completed merge document with variables from the data source.

The Benefits of Using Mail Merge

Mail Merge saves a lot of time. For example, imagine you want to send a letter to 100 customers. Without Mail Merge, you would have to type the same text in all 100 letters (or copy and paste 100 times). However, with Mail Merge, you create one main document with the standard text and one data source containing customer names and addresses.

You will also really appreciate Mail Merge when you later decide you want to make a change. Using Mail Merge, you can edit the main document once and remerge it with the data source to produce a new merged document. Without Mail Merge, you would need to edit each letter individually.

The Mailings Tab

The Mailings tab provides guidance in setting up both the main document and data source, and it helps you conduct the merge. The Start Mail Merge group is the beginning point. Alternatively, you can choose Step-by-Step Mail Merge Wizard from the Start Mail Merge menu to walk you through the process.

You specify the type of document (letters, envelopes, or labels) here.

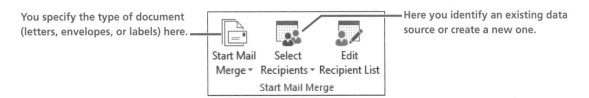

Here you identify an existing data source or create a new one.

Working with the Data Source

Video Library   http://labyrinthelab.com/videos   Video Number: WD13-V0702

Data sources typically contain names, addresses, telephone numbers, and other contact information. However, you can include any information in a data source. For example, you could include part numbers and prices to create a parts catalog. You can create a data source in Word, or you can use an external data source, such as an Access or Excel database. Once a data source is created, it can be merged with many different main documents.

Designing Effective Data Sources

It is important to design effective data sources. The most important consideration is the number of fields—the more fields, the more flexibility. You cannot merge a portion of a field. If a field contains both a first and last name, for example, you would not be able to merge the last name without the first name into a greeting line such as *Dear Ms. Alvarez*. In this example, you would need to use one field for the first name and a separate field for the last name. You would also need to use a field for titles (Mr., Ms., and Mrs.). This guideline is not critical if you know you will not use the data source again and the main document does not require this flexibility.

Creating a New Address List

You can use the New Address List dialog box to set up address lists (data sources) for mail merges. This tool stores the addresses in a table in a Microsoft Access database. Each row in the table is referred to as a record. This table, which becomes the data source for the merge, is connected to the mail merge main document.

The dialog box contains predefined columns (fields).

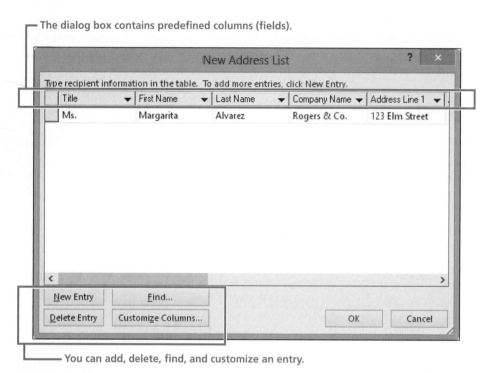

You can add, delete, find, and customize an entry.

Customizing an Address List

The Customize Address List dialog box allows you to modify the predefined columns. It's easy to set up the mailing list just as you want it.

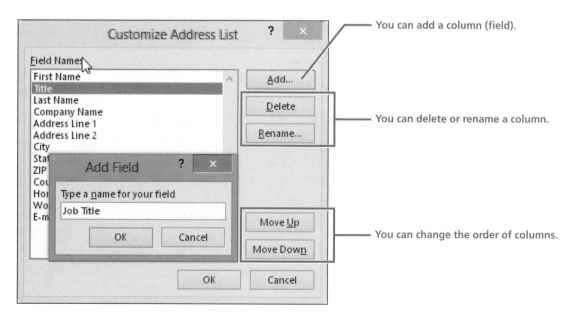

You can add a column (field).

You can delete or rename a column.

You can change the order of columns.

Specify the Main Document and Create a Data Source

In this exercise, you will use the Start Mail Merge group to specify a letter as your main document, to customize the data source, and to enter data.

1. Start **Word**. Open **WD07-D01-SalesLetter** from your **WD2013 Lesson 07** folder and save it as `WD07-D01-SalesLetter-[FirstInitialLastName]`.

   Replace the bracketed text with your first initial and last name. For example, if your name is Bethany Smith, your filename would look like this: WD07-D01-SalesLetter-BSmith.

2. Choose **Mailings→Start Mail Merge→Start Mail Merge** 📄 **→Letters**.

   You are indicating that the letter you just opened will be the main document. Now you will create your mailing list.

3. Choose **Mailings→Start Mail Merge→Select Recipients** 📇 **→Type a New List**.

   The New Address List dialog box opens. Now you will remove unnecessary fields and add a new field.

4. Click **Customize Columns** to open the Customize Address List dialog box.

5. Choose **Address Line 2** and click **Delete**; click **Yes** to verify the deletion.

6. Delete **Country or Region**, **Home Phone**, **Work Phone**, and **E-mail Address**, and then click **Title** at the top of the list.

7. Follow these steps to add a field:

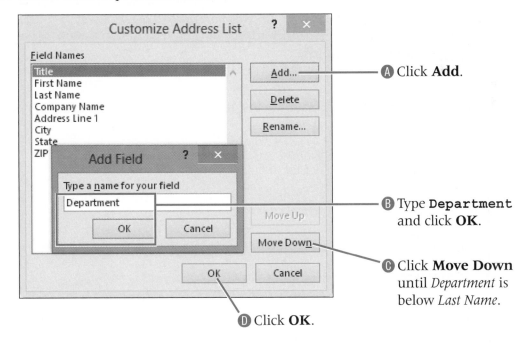

Ⓐ Click **Add**.

Ⓑ Type **Department** and click **OK**.

Ⓒ Click **Move Down** until *Department* is below *Last Name*.

Ⓓ Click **OK**.

Enter Records

The insertion point should be in the Title field.

8. Follow these steps to begin the first record:

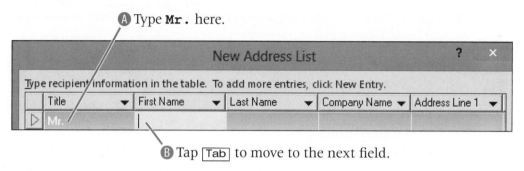

Ⓐ Type **Mr.** here.

Ⓑ Tap `Tab` to move to the next field.

Do not type spaces after entering information in a field. Word takes care of adding the necessary spaces. You can click a field and make editing changes if necessary.

9. Type **Talos** and tap `Tab` to move to the next field.

10. Finish entering the Talos Bouras data shown here, tapping `Tab` between fields. The list of fields will scroll as you `Tab` and type.

11. When you complete the first record, click **New Entry** or tap `Tab` to generate a new row for the next record; then, enter the two remaining records shown.

Mr. Talos Bouras	Ms. Nicole Romero	Mr. Michael Chowdrey
Administration	Maintenance	Operations
Conrad Corporation	Harris Health Services	Seligman Enterprises
854 Whitmore Drive	132 Lake Street	900 C Street
San Diego CA 92101	San Diego CA 92101	La Jolla CA 92103

If you accidentally tap `Tab` after the last record, just click Delete Entry to remove the blank record.

12. Leave the **New Address List** dialog box open.

Reviewing Your Records

Video Library   http://labyrinthelab.com/videos   Video Number: WD13-V0703

It's a good idea to review your records for accuracy before saving the data source. However, if you miss an error, you can always edit it later.

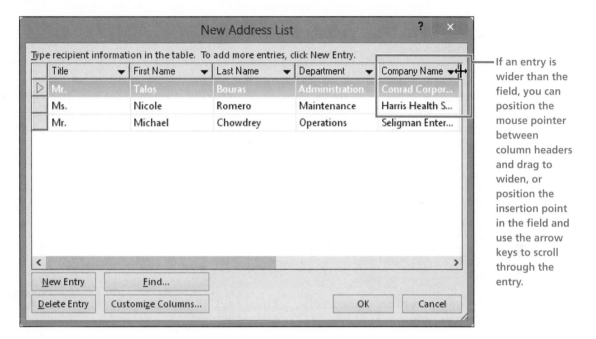

If an entry is wider than the field, you can position the mouse pointer between column headers and drag to widen, or position the insertion point in the field and use the arrow keys to scroll through the entry.

DEVELOP YOUR SKILLS WD07-D02

Review and Save Your Work

In this exercise, you will examine your records for accuracy and save your data source.

1. Position the mouse pointer on the scroll bar at the bottom of the dialog box, and drag left and right to view all the fields.

2. Follow these steps to review your records:

Ⓐ Position the insertion point here and use the arrow keys to move through the entry.

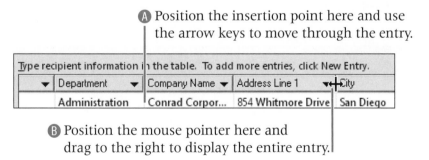

Ⓑ Position the mouse pointer here and drag to the right to display the entire entry.

3. Correct any typos.

4. When you finish reviewing your records, click **OK** to open the Save Address List dialog box.

5. Save the data source file as `WD07-D02-SalesLtrData-[FirstInitialLastName]` in the **WD2013 Lesson 07** folder.

   Your data source is now connected to the main document.

Managing the Address List

Video Library   http://labyrinthelab.com/videos   Video Number: WD13-V0704

The Mail Merge Recipients dialog box lets you sort and filter address lists and choose records to include in a mail merge. To edit data, you use the Edit Data Source dialog box to add, delete, and edit entries. If you used a Word table, Excel spreadsheet, or other document for your data source, you can edit directly in that data source document.

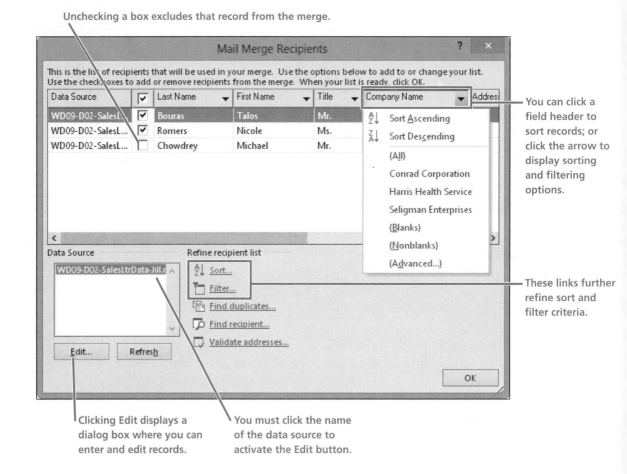

Unchecking a box excludes that record from the merge.

You can click a field header to sort records; or click the arrow to display sorting and filtering options.

These links further refine sort and filter criteria.

Clicking Edit displays a dialog box where you can enter and edit records.

You must click the name of the data source to activate the Edit button.

Use Recipient Options and Edit Records

In this exercise, you will work with the Mail Merge Recipients dialog box, where you can sort, filter, and edit your mailing list.

1. Choose **Mailings→Start Mail Merge→Edit Recipient List** .

2. Follow these steps to sort and filter the list and open the Edit Data Source dialog box:

Ⓐ Click this field header to sort the list in ascending order by last name.

Ⓑ Click the drop-down arrow and choose **Chowdery** to filter out other entries. Click the arrow again and choose **(All)** to redisplay all records.

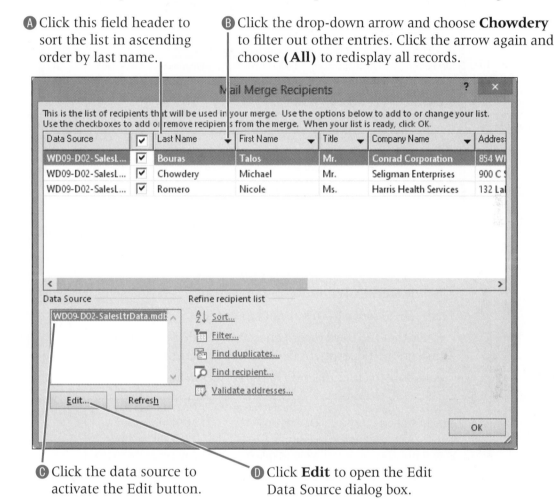

Ⓒ Click the data source to activate the Edit button.

Ⓓ Click **Edit** to open the Edit Data Source dialog box.

Edit a Record

The Edit Data Source dialog box looks and operates like the New Address List dialog box.

3. Follow these steps to edit a record:

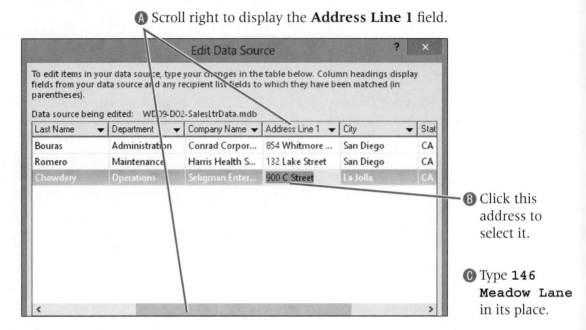

Ⓐ Scroll right to display the **Address Line 1** field.

Ⓑ Click this address to select it.

Ⓒ Type **146 Meadow Lane** in its place.

4. Follow these guidelines to enter the three records in the following illustration:
   - Use the **New Entry** button or tap Tab at the end of each row for each new record.
   - Tap Tab to move from one field to the next.
   - Notice that the third record does not include a department name. Tap Tab to pass through the Department field and leave it empty.
   - Make sure to enter the data in the correct fields.

Ms. Mary Wright	Mr. Derek Navarro	Mr. Andre Adams
Administration	Operations	Mills Insurance
Rogers Electric Company	Gourmet Warehouse	2224 Culver Drive
1240 Potrero Avenue	3300 Maple Drive	San Diego CA 92102
San Diego CA 92101	La Jolla CA 92103	

5. Click **OK** to close the dialog box.

6. Click **Yes** when the message appears verifying your update.
   Notice your changes in the Mail Merge Recipients dialog box.

7. Click **OK** to close the Mail Merge Recipients dialog box.

Working with Main Documents

Video Library   http://labyrinthelab.com/videos   Video Number: WD13-V0705

You accomplish a merge by combining a main document with a data source. A main document is attached to a data source that includes one or more merge fields. Merge fields in a main document correspond to fields in the data source. Some merge codes, such as the Address Block code, are composite fields consisting of a number of grouped fields. For example, Title, First Name, Last Name, Address, City, State, and Zip would be included in the Address Block code.

When you conduct a merge, a customized letter, envelope, or label is created for each record in the data source. The following figure shows the command buttons in the Write & Insert Fields group that you use to insert merge fields into your document.

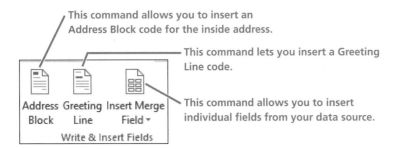

This command allows you to insert an Address Block code for the inside address.

This command lets you insert a Greeting Line code.

This command allows you to insert individual fields from your data source.

719 Coronado Drive
San Diego, California 92102

Today's Date

«AddressBlock»

«GreetingLine»

Green Clean is a locally owned and operated commercial janitorial service. Our employees are highly trained, and our supervisors check on every job every night to ensure the best quality work.

We follow all EPA guidelines and comply with OSHA standards. We use only environmentally safe cleaning products, providing you with a healthy, nontoxic, clean place of business.

Good customer service is our number one priority. Our proactive account managers stay in touch with our clients and follow through on all requests. We have been in business over twenty years and we have scores of long-term clients.

«First_Name», one of our account managers will contact you in the near future to discuss you janitorial needs.

Sincerely,

Ahn Tran
President

Here is a form letter with the merge fields inserted. When you execute the merge, the Address Block, Greeting Line, and First Name codes are replaced with information from the data source.

Set Up a Form Letter

In this exercise, you will set up a form letter. The sales letter main document should still be open.

1. If necessary, choose **Home→Paragraph→Show/Hide** ¶ to display formatting characters.

2. Select the **Today's Date** line and tap ⎡Delete⎤.

3. Choose **Insert→Text→Insert Date and Time** 📅 .

4. Choose the third date format, check **Update Automatically**, and click **OK**.

   Checking the Update Automatically option means the date in your letter will always be the current date, which is a convenient option for form letters that you want to use again.

5. Tap ⎡Enter⎤ four times after inserting the date.

   Now you will insert the Address Block code.

6. Choose **Mailings→Write & Insert Fields→Address Block** 📄 .

   The Insert Address Block dialog box allows you to choose a format for the address block.

7. Follow these steps to insert an Address Block code:

   A Choose different formats and view the preview on the right; then choose **Mr. Joshua Randall Jr**.

   B Leave the remaining options as shown and click **OK**.

The <<AddressBlock>> code appears in the letter. During the merge, Word will insert inside address information from the data source at the Address Block code location.

8. Tap Enter twice.

Now you will insert the Greeting Line code.

9. Choose **Mailings→Write & Insert Fields→Greeting Line** 📄.

10. Follow these steps to modify and insert the Greeting Line code:

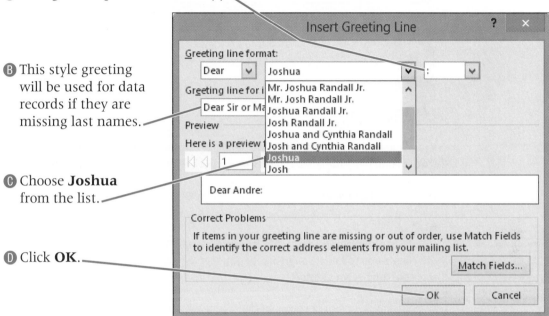

Ⓐ Change this option to a **colon (:)**.

Ⓑ This style greeting will be used for data records if they are missing last names.

Ⓒ Choose **Joshua** from the list.

Ⓓ Click **OK**.

11. Tap Enter twice.

12. Follow these steps to insert the First Name code into the letter:

Ⓑ Click the **Insert Merge Field** menu button ▼.

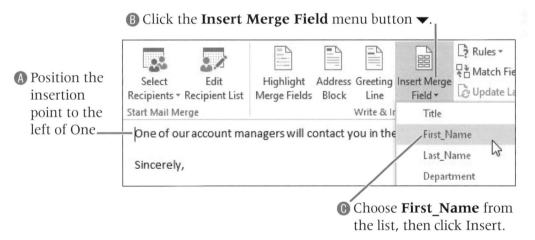

Ⓐ Position the insertion point to the left of One

Ⓒ Choose **First_Name** from the list, then click Insert.

13. Close the Insert Merge Field dialog box.

14. Type a comma and tap Spacebar; then delete the **uppercase O** and replace it with a **lowercase o**.

15. Take a few moments to review your letter, making sure the merge fields match this example. In particular, make sure you used the proper punctuation and spacing between fields and the text.

The merge fields are highlighted in the following illustration to help you locate them; your merge fields do not need to be highlighted. (The Highlight Merge Fields button is in the Write & Insert Fields group.)

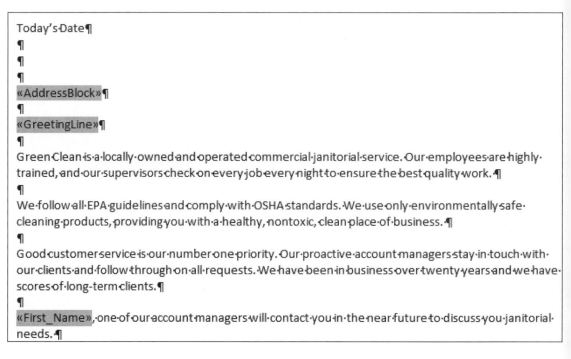

 Any punctuation or spacing errors that occur in your main document will appear in every merged letter.

16. Choose **Home→Paragraph→Show/Hide** ¶ to turn off formatting marks.

17. Save your file.

Conducting a Merge

Video Library http://labyrinthelab.com/videos Video Number: WD13-V0706

Merging combines a main document with a data source document. If you are merging a form letter with a data source, Word produces a personalized copy of the form letter for each record in the data source.

Previewing the Results

It's always a good idea to preview the merge results before you complete the merge so you can make corrections if needed. If you notice an error that needs to be fixed in the main document, simply click the Preview Results button again to return to the main document.

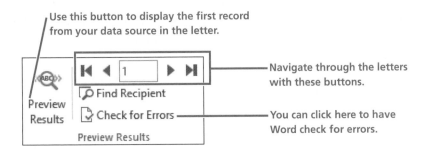

Use this button to display the first record from your data source in the letter.

Navigate through the letters with these buttons.

You can click here to have Word check for errors.

Using "Check for Errors"

When you have many records to preview, rather than previewing each one individually, you can use Check for Errors. Word goes through the document checking for common errors, such as an invalid field code. In the Checking and Reporting Errors dialog box, you have three options for viewing errors.

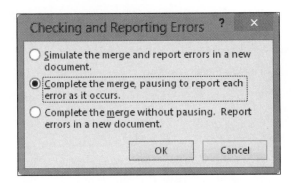

Finishing the Merge

When you feel confident that your letter and data source are accurate, you use the Finish & Merge command.

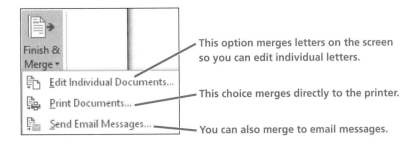

This option merges letters on the screen so you can edit individual letters.

This choice merges directly to the printer.

You can also merge to email messages.

To Save or Not to Save

Merged documents are rarely saved because they can easily be reconstructed by merging the main document with the data source. Instead, merged documents are usually previewed, printed, and closed without saving. But you can certainly save the merged document if you wish to have a record of it. If a merged document contains errors, you can close it without saving, edit the main document or data source, and conduct the merge again.

Task	Procedure
Specify the main document	▪ Choose Mailings→Start Mail Merge→Start Mail Merge; specify the main document type.
Create data source	▪ Choose Mailings→Start Mail Merge→Select Recipients; choose the data source option.
Customize data source	▪ Choose Mailings→Start Mail Merge→Select Recipients, choose Type a New List, and click Customize Columns.
Sort and filter data source	▪ Choose Mailings→Start Mail Merge→Edit Recipient List. ▪ Click the drop-down arrow in the column header; choose the sort option or filter item.
Edit data source	▪ Choose Mailings→Start Mail Merge→Edit Recipient List, click the data source, and click Edit.
Insert merge codes in main document	▪ Position the insertion point where the merge code should appear. ▪ Choose Mailings→Write & Insert Fields, and then choose Address Block, Greeting Line, or Insert Merge Field.
Preview results	▪ Choose Mailings→Preview Results→Preview Results.
Conduct a merge	▪ Choose Mailings→Finish→Finish & Merge; choose the result.

Conduct a Merge

In this exercise, you will use the Preview Results commands to review your letters. Then you will complete the merge on the screen.

1. Follow these steps to preview the merge:

   Ⓐ Click **Preview Results** to display the first inside address.

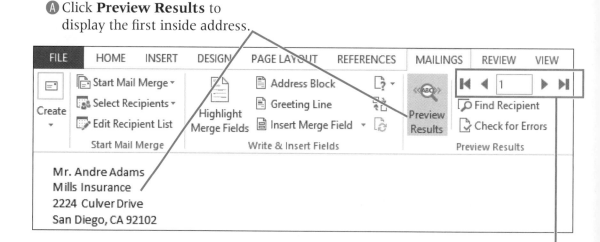

   Ⓑ Use the navigation buttons to scroll through all of your merged documents.

2. Choose **Mailings→Finish→Finish & Merge** 📄→**Edit Individual Documents** to merge the letters on the screen.

3. Click **OK** to merge all records.

4. Scroll through the letters and scan their contents.

   Notice that there is one letter for each record in the data source.

5. Close the merged document without saving.

6. Choose **Mailings→Preview Results→Preview Results** 🔍 again to display the main document instead of the preview.

Working with Merge Problems

| Video Library | http://labyrinthelab.com/videos | Video Number: WD13-V0707 |

Several common errors can cause a merge to produce incorrect results. The merged document (or preview) will usually provide clues as to why a merge fails to produce the intended results. Once you identify an error in the merged document, such as leaving out a comma or space before or after a merge field, you can make changes to the main document. You can also edit the data source. You can then conduct the merge again to determine if the error was fixed. Repeat this process until the merge works as intended.

Solving Common Merge Problems

Several problems are common in merges. These problems and their solutions are described in the following Quick Reference table.

COMMON MERGE PROBLEMS	
Problem	**Solution**
The same error appears in *every* merge letter.	The problem is in the main document. Correct the error and perform the merge again.
Some letters are missing data.	Some records in the data source are missing data. Add data and perform the merge again.
Some letters have incorrect data.	Some records in the data source are incorrect. Correct the errors, and perform the merge again.

DEVELOP YOUR SKILLS WD07-D06
Fix Merge Problems

In this exercise, you will examine your document for merge problems. This exercise does not address all possible merge problems; it does, however, address one specific error that you will make intentionally. You will insert a colon after the Greeting Line code.

1. Position the insertion point after **<<GreetingLine>>** and type a colon.

2. Choose **Mailings→Finish→Finish & Merge→Edit Individual Documents**.

3. Click **OK** to merge all records.

4. Browse through the merged document and notice that there are two colons following the greeting line in *every* letter.

   Because the error occurs in every letter, you know the error is in the main document.

5. Locate any other errors and notice how often the errors occur (in every merged letter or just one).

   Next you will correct the double colon error and any other errors you discovered that occurred in all letters.

6. Close the merged document without saving; then, edit and save the main document.

7. Follow these guidelines if you find a data error in *just one letter*.

   ▪ Choose **Mailings→Start Mail Merge→Edit Recipient List** 📝.

   ▪ In the Mail Merge Recipients dialog box, highlight the **Data Source** in the bottom-left corner, and click **Edit**.

   ▪ Fix any errors and click **OK**; click **Yes** to update the data.

   ▪ Click **OK** to close the dialog box.

8. When you have corrected any errors, execute the merge again.

9. Close the merged document without saving it.

10. Save and close the sales letter main document.

Merging Envelopes and Labels

Video Library   http://labyrinthelab.com/videos   Video Number: WD13-V0708

When you begin a mail merge, Word presents you with options for the type of main document you can create. In addition to form letters, you can choose envelopes, labels, and other types of documents. You can use the same data source for various main documents. For example, you can use the same data source for envelopes and mailing labels that you used for the form letter.

Generating Envelopes with Mail Merge

Mail Merge lets you choose the envelope size and formats. The standard business (Size 10) envelope is the default. Check your printer manual for instructions on loading envelopes.

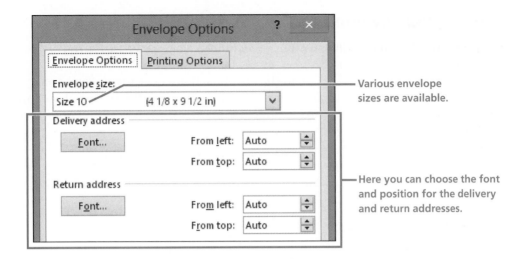

Various envelope sizes are available.

Here you can choose the font and position for the delivery and return addresses.

DEVELOP YOUR SKILLS WD07-D07

Choose an Envelope Size and Attach a Data Source

In this exercise, you will choose an envelope as the main document and connect the sales letter data file to the envelope.

1. Start a new blank document.

2. Choose **Mailings→Start Mail Merge→Start Mail Merge** →**Envelopes**.

3. In the Envelope Options dialog box, if necessary, choose **Size 10** as the Envelope Size and click **OK**.

   Now you will attach the data source that you used for your letter.

4. Choose **Mailings→Start Mail Merge→Select Recipients** →**Use an Existing List**.

5. In the Select Data Source dialog box, navigate to your **WD2013 Lesson 07** folder and open **WD07-D02-SalesLtrData-[FirstInitialLastName]**.

Arranging the Envelope

Video Library   http://labyrinthelab.com/videos   Video Number: WD13-V0709

You can insert an Address Block code in the envelope main document. You save an envelope main document like any other main document. The following illustration shows an envelope main document.

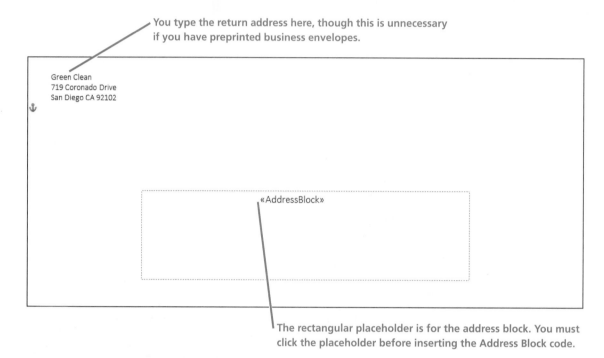

You type the return address here, though this is unnecessary if you have preprinted business envelopes.

Green Clean
719 Coronado Drive
San Diego CA 92102

«AddressBlock»

The rectangular placeholder is for the address block. You must click the placeholder before inserting the Address Block code.

DEVELOP YOUR SKILLS WD07-D08
Merge to Envelopes

In this exercise, you will place the return address and the address block code on the envelope. You will also merge the envelope main document with the data source.

1. If necessary, choose **Home→Paragraph→Show/Hide** ¶ to turn on formatting marks.

2. Type the following return address starting at the first paragraph symbol in the upper-left corner of the envelope.

   ```
   Green Clean
   719 Coronado Drive
   San Diego CA 92102
   ```

3. Position the insertion point next to the paragraph symbol toward the center of the envelope.

4. Choose **Mailings→Write & Insert Fields→Address Block** 📄 .

5. Click **OK** to accept the default address block settings.

   Word will merge the address information from the data source into this location when you perform the merge. First, you will preview the merge.

6. Choose **Mailings→Preview Results→Preview Results** 🔍 to display a record from the data source in the envelope.

7. Use the navigation buttons in the Preview Results group to scroll through all of your merged envelopes.

8. Choose **Mailings→Finish→Finish & Merge** 📄→**Edit Individual Documents** and click **OK** to merge all records.

9. Choose **Home→Paragraph→Show/Hide** ¶ to turn off formatting marks.

10. Scroll through the envelopes, and notice that there is one envelope for each record in the data source.

    You could use the envelopes for mailing the letters created in the previous exercises, because they are generated from the same data source.

11. If necessary, fix any problems with the mail merge and merge the envelopes again.

12. When you finish, close the merged document without saving it.

13. Choose **Mailings→Preview Results→Preview Results** 🔍 to turn off the preview.

14. Save the main document envelope as **WD07-D08-SalesLtrEnv-[FirstInitialLastName]** in your **WD2013 Lesson 07** folder; close the document.

Generating Labels with Mail Merge

Video Library   http://labyrinthelab.com/videos   Video Number: WD13-V0710

You can use Mail Merge to generate mailing labels for each record in a data source. Mail Merge lets you choose the label format, sheet size, and other specifications. It also lets you insert an Address Block code and other codes in the main document. Like other main documents, a labels main document can be saved for future use. The following illustration shows a portion of the labels main document that you will set up.

«AddressBlock»	«Next Record»«AddressBlock»	«Next Record»«AddressBlock»
«Next Record»«AddressBlock»	«Next Record»«AddressBlock»	«Next Record»«AddressBlock»
«Next Record»«AddressBlock»	«Next Record»«AddressBlock»	«Next Record»«AddressBlock»

Using Label Options

The Label Options dialog box allows you to choose printer options and the type of label you will use. You will find a number on the package of labels you purchase that may correspond to the Product Number in the Label Options dialog box. If you buy a brand name not included in the Label Vendors list, you can match your label size with the label size in the Label Information section.

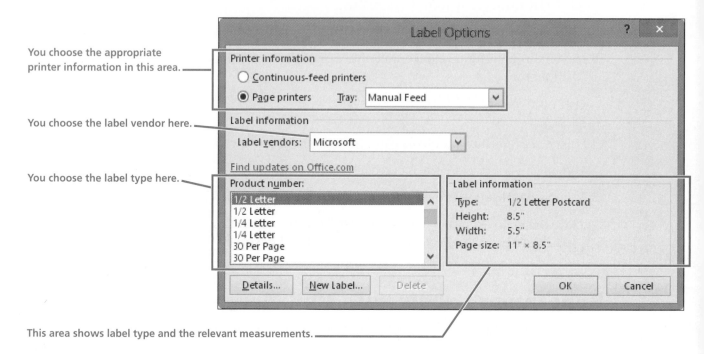

You choose the appropriate printer information in this area.

You choose the label vendor here.

You choose the label type here.

This area shows label type and the relevant measurements.

Use Mail Merge to Generate Mailing Labels

In this exercise, you will set up a labels main document and merge it with the data source used in the previous exercises.

1. Start a new blank document.

2. If necessary, choose **Home→Paragraph→Show/Hide** ¶ to display formatting marks.

3. Choose **Mailings→Start Mail Merge→Start Mail Merge** ▤ →**Labels**.

4. Follow these steps to choose a printer option and a label:

Ⓐ Choose **Default Tray**. Ⓑ Choose **Avery US Letter**.

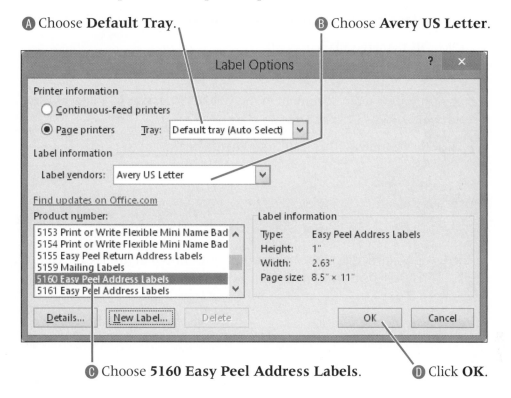

Ⓒ Choose **5160 Easy Peel Address Labels**. Ⓓ Click **OK**.

The labels main document appears in the Word window. Labels are contained in a Word table, but don't worry, you don't have to be a table expert to create labels.

Connect the Data Source

5. Choose **Mailings→Start Mail Merge→Select Recipients** ▣ **→Use an Existing List**.

6. In the Select Data Source dialog box, navigate to your **WD2013 Lesson 07** folder and open **WD07-D02-SalesLtrData-[FirstInitialLastName]**.

7. Make sure the insertion point is next to the paragraph symbol in the first address label.
Notice that the space for the first label is blank and all the rest have a Next Record code in them. Now you will add the Address Block code.

8. Choose **Mailings→Write & Insert Fields→Address Block** ▤ and click **OK**.

9. Choose **Mailings→Write & Insert Fields→Update Labels** ▣ to place the Address Block code in all labels.
Your addresses will fit the labels better if you remove Word's additional spacing.

10. Select the table.

11. Choose **Page Layout→Paragraph**, type **0** in the **Before Spacing** field, and tap Enter.

12. Choose **Mailings→Preview Results→Preview Results** ▣ to see how the labels will look when you print them. Turn off Preview Results when you are finished.

Conduct the Merge

13. Choose **Mailings→Finish→Finish & Merge** 🖹→**Edit Individual Documents**.

14. Click **OK** to merge all the records.

15. Close your merged document without saving it.

16. Save the labels main document in the **WD2013 Lesson 07** folder as `WD07-D09-MergeLabels-[FirstInitialLastName]`.

17. Close the document, then exit from **Word**.

Concepts Review

To check your knowledge of the key concepts introduced in this lesson, complete the Concepts Review quiz by choosing the appropriate access option below.

If you are...	Then access the quiz by...
Using the Labyrinth Video Library	Going to http://labyrinthelab.com/videos
Using eLab	Logging in, choosing Content, and navigating to the Concepts Review quiz for this lesson
Not using the Labyrinth Video Library or eLab	Going to the student resource center for this book

Reinforce Your Skills

Create a Data Source and Main Document

In this exercise, you will create a data source and main document for a Kids for Change mailing. The kids are holding a fundraiser for a micro-lending project that focuses on poor people in India. They will conduct a mailing to announce the upcoming project and canvass their neighborhoods for donations.

Work with a Data Source

1. Start **Word**. Open **WD07-R01-Fundraiser** from your **WD2013 Lesson 07** folder and save it as `WD07-R01-FundRaiser-[FirstInitialLastName]`.

2. Choose **Mailings→Start Mail Merge→Start Mail Merge→Letters** to identify the fund raising letter as the main document.

3. Choose **Mailings→Start Mail Merge→Select Recipients** ▦ **→Type a New List**.
   Now you will customize the list of fields.

4. Click **Customize Columns**.

5. Click **Address Line 2** and click **Delete**.

6. Click **Yes** to confirm the deletion.

7. Also delete the following fields:
   - Country or Region
   - Home Phone
   - Work Phone
   - E-mail Address

   Now you will rename a field.

8. Click **Address Line 1** and click **Rename**.

9. Delete everything except *Address* and click **OK**.

Now you will add two fields.

10. Click **Zip Code** and click **Add**.

11. Type `Member Last Name` in the Add Field dialog box and click **OK**.

12. Also add a field called `Member First Name`.

    Next you will move a field.

13. Click **Member Last Name**, click **Move Down** once, and click **OK** to position Member First Name above Member Last Name.

14. Make sure the insertion point is in the **Title** field, type `Ms.`, and tap `Tab`.

15. Type `Loretta` in the First Name field and tap `Tab`.

16. Continue typing and tabbing to complete the first record shown here. Be sure to include the member first name, Eric, and last name, Speck, in the first record.

Ms. Loretta Morales Morales Super Market 311 Ocean Street Miami FL 33130	Mr. Tony D'Agusto Tony's Trattoria 675 Miller Ave. Miami FL 33129	Mr. Allan Morgan 951 4th Street Miami FL 33136	Ms. Margarita Elizondo Elan Fashions 307 Dolphin Way Miami FL 33136
Member: Eric Speck	**Member:** Wendy Chang	**Member:** Stella Hopkins	**Member:** Diego Cantero

17. Tap `Tab` to begin a new record.

18. Continue typing and tabbing to enter the next three records shown in step 16.

19. Be sure to skip the **Company** field for the third record.

20. Review your records for accuracy; click **OK** when you are satisfied with your work.

21. Save the data source in your **WD2013 Lesson 07** folder as `WD07-R01-FundraiserData-[FirstInitialLastName]`.

    Your fundraiser letter should be on the screen.

Set Up the Main Document

22. If necessary, choose **Home→Paragraph→Show/Hide ¶** to display formatting marks.

23. In the fundraiser letter, select **[Inside Address]** but not the paragraph symbol at the end of the line and tap `Delete`.

24. Choose **Mailings→Write & Insert Fields→Address Block** 📄, and then click **OK** to accept the default address block settings.

25. Delete **[Name]** in the greeting line, but not the paragraph symbol at the end of the line.

26. Choose **Mailings→Write & Insert Fields→Greeting Line** 📄.

27. Choose **Joshua** and colon in the Greeting Line Format area as shown and click **OK**.

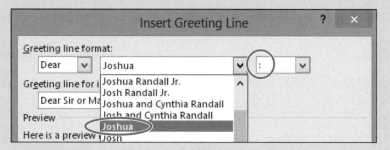

28. In the last sentence of the first paragraph, delete **[Member Name]**.

29. Choose **Mailings→Write & Insert Fields→Insert Merge Field** 📄 **menu button ▼→Member_First_Name**.

30. Tap ⎵Spacebar⎵ and insert the Member_Last_Name field, then close the dialog box.

31. Save and close the letter; exit from **Word**.

32. Submit your final files based on the guidelines provided by your instructor.

To view examples of how your file or files should look at the end of this exercise, go to the student resource center.

REINFORCE YOUR SKILLS WD07-R02
Merge a Letter, Envelopes, and Labels

In this exercise, you will merge a data source with a letter and work with a merge problem. You will also merge the data source with envelopes and labels.

Conduct a Merge and Preview Results

1. Start **Word**. Open **WD07-R02-ParentLtr** from your **WD2013 Lesson 07** folder and save it as `WD07-R02-ParentLtr-[FirstInitialLastName]`.

2. Choose **Mailings→Start Mail Merge→Start Mail Merge→Letters**.

3. Choose **Mailings→Start Mail Merge→Select Recipients** 📇 **→Use an Existing List**.

4. Navigate to your **WD2013 Lesson 07** folder and open **WD07-R02-ParentData**.

5. Choose **Mailings→Preview Results→Preview Results** 🔍 to preview the first record.
Notice that the greeting line is incorrect.

6. Preview all three records, and notice that the greeting line is incorrect in all.
This indicates that the error is in the main document.

7. Choose **Mailings→Preview Results→Preview Results** 🔍 to turn off the preview.

Fix Merge Problems and Complete the Merge

8. In the greeting line, delete *Dear* and the space that follows it; then delete the colon at the end of the greeting line.

   Dear and the punctuation at the end of the greeting line are included in the Greeting Line code.

9. Choose **Mailings→Preview Results→Preview Results** 🔍 .

   Notice that the greeting line is now correctly formatted.

   Notice the child's name (Aiden, in the first record) has no spaces around it.

10. Choose **Mailings→Preview Results→Preview Results** 🔍 to return to the main document, and then insert a space before and after the **Child Name** code.

11. Preview the letter again and notice that the **Child Name** variable is correctly spaced.

12. Make sure the spacing between the address block and the greeting line and between the greeting line and the first paragraph are correct.

13. Turn off **Preview Results** 🔍 , and make any changes necessary.

14. Choose **Mailings→Finish→Finish & Merge** 📄 **→Edit Individual Documents**, and then click **OK** to merge all records.

15. Scroll through the merged letters; close the file without saving it.

16. Save and close the parent letter main document.

Generate an Envelope

17. Start a new blank document.

18. Choose **Mailings→Start Mail Merge→Start Mail Merge** 📄 **→Envelopes**.

19. Click **OK** to accept the envelope options defaults.

20. Choose **Mailings→Start Mail Merge→Select Recipients** 📇 **→Use an Existing List**.

21. Navigate to your **WD2013 Lesson 07** folder and open **WD07-R02-ParentData** to attach the data source to the envelope.

22. If necessary, choose **Home→Paragraph→Show/Hide** ¶ to display formatting marks.

23. Type the following return address at the first paragraph symbol in the upper-left corner of the envelope.

    ```
    Kids for Change
    726 Throckmorton Ave.
    Sacramento CA 95612
    ```

24. Click the insertion point next to the paragraph symbol toward the center of the envelope.

25. Choose **Mailings→Write & Insert Fields→Address Block** 📄 .

26. Click **OK** to accept the address block default formats.

27. Choose **Mailings→Preview Results→Preview Results** 🔍 .

28. Navigate through all three records to ensure they appear correctly on the envelope.

29. Turn off **Preview Results** 📖 .

30. Save the envelope as `WD07-R02-ParentEnv-[FirstInitialLastName]` in your **WD2013 Lesson 07** folder; close the envelope file.

Generate Mailing Labels

31. Start a new blank document.

32. Choose **Mailings→Start Mail Merge→Start Mail Merge→** 📇 **Labels**.

33. Choose **Avery US Letter** as the Label Vendor, choose **5160 Easy Peel Address Labels** as the Product Number, and click **OK**.

34. If necessary, choose **Home→Paragraph→Show/Hide** ¶ to display formatting marks.

35. Choose **Mailings→Start Mail Merge→Select Recipients** 📇 **→Use an Existing List**.

36. Navigate to your **WD2013 Lesson 07** folder and open **WD07-R02-ParentData**.

37. Make sure the insertion point is next to the paragraph symbol in the first label.

38. Choose **Mailings→Write & Insert Fields→Address Block** 📄 .

39. Click **OK** to accept the address block defaults.

40. Choose **Mailings→Write & Insert Fields→Update Labels** 📋 to insert the Address Block code on all labels.

41. Choose **Mailings→Preview Results→Preview Results** 📖 to verify that the labels will print correctly.

    Because these addresses are three-line addresses, they fit on the Avery 5160 labels without removing Word's extra spacing.

42. Turn off **Preview Results** 📖 to return to the labels main document.

43. Save the labels file as `WD07-R02-ParentLabels-[FirstInitialLastName]` in your **WD2013 Lesson 07** folder. Close the file and exit from **Word**.

44. Submit your final files based on the guidelines provided by your instructor.

    To view examples of how your file or files should look at the end of this exercise, go to the student resource center.

REINFORCE YOUR SKILLS WD07-R03

Merge a Letter, Envelopes, and Labels

In this exercise, you will create a data source and a main document. Then you will preview the results and correct any merge problems before conducting the merge. Finally, you will generate envelopes and mailing labels.

Create a Data Source

1. Start **Word**. Open **WD07-R03-Walkers** from your **WD2013 Lesson 07** folder and save it as `WD07-R03-Walkers-[FirstInitialLastName]`.

2. Choose **Mailings→Start Mail Merge→Start Mail Merge** 📄 **→Letters** to designate the Walkers letter as the main document.

3. Choose **Mailings→Start Mail Merge→Select Recipients** 🖼 →**Type a New List**.
   Now you will customize the data source columns.

4. Click **Customize Columns** to display the Customize Address List dialog box.

5. Click **Company Name** and click **Delete**; click **Yes** to confirm the deletion.

6. Delete the following fields:
   - Address Line 2
   - Country or Region
   - Work Phone
   - E-mail Address

7. Click **Address Line 1** and click **Rename**.

8. Delete everything except the word *Address* and click **OK** twice.

9. Ensure the insertion point is in the **Title** field, type **Mr.**, and tap ⌨Tab to move to the next field.

10. Type **Sean** in the **First Name** field, tap ⌨Tab, and type **Corn** in the **Last Name** field.

11. Continue tabbing and typing to complete the Sean Corn record as shown.

Mr. Sean Corn 308 Alhambra Avenue Monterey CA 93940 831-555-1234	Mr. Craig Dostie 31200 Erwin Street Monterey CA 93940 831-555-4567	Ms. Alexia Lopez 2134 Harbor Blvd. Monterey CA 93942 831-555-9632
Ms. Margaret Wong 1308 West Ramona Blvd. Monterey CA 93940 831-555-1598	Ms. Phyllis Coen 4745 Buffin Avenue Monterey CA 93943 831-555-3578	Mr. Winston Boey 263 East Howard Street Monterey CA 93944 831-555-7896

12. Either tap ⌨Tab or click **New Entry** to begin the next record, and finish entering the remaining records in the table.

13. Review your records for accuracy.
    Now you will sort your list by Last Name.

14. Click the **Last Name** column header to sort the list alphabetically in ascending order.

15. Click **OK**; then, navigate to your **WD2013 Lesson 07** and save the file as **WD07-R03-WalkerData-[FirstInitialLastName]**.

Title ▼	First Name ▼	Last Name ▼
Mr.	Winston	Boey
Ms	Phyllis	Coen
Mr.	Sean	Corn
Mr.	Craig	Dostie
Ms.	Alexia	Lopez
Ms.	Margaret	Wong

Set Up the Main Document

16. Replace *INSIDE ADDRESS* with the **Address Block** code using the default formats.

17. Replace *GREETING LINE* with the **Greeting Line** code, changing the Greeting Line Format name to **Joshua**.

18. In the last paragraph, replace *HOME PHONE* with the **Home Phone** code.

Conduct the Merge and Preview Results

19. Preview your letters and correct any errors in the main document, paying particular attention to spacing.

    ■ There should be a blank line between the inside address and the greeting line, and between the greeting line and the body of the letter.

    ■ There should be a space before the home phone.

Work with Merge Problems

20. Turn off **Preview Results** 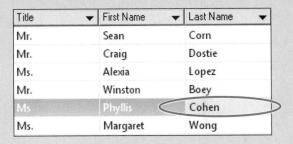 and make any changes necessary to the main document.
    Phyllis Cohen's name is misspelled. You will make that correction now.

21. Choose **Mailings→Start Mail Merge→Edit Recipient List** .

22. Click the data source in the bottom-left corner and click **Edit**.

23. Change the spelling from *Coen* to **Cohen**.

24. Click **OK**; click **Yes** to verify the update and then click **OK** again.

25. Preview the results again to verify the change to the data source and any changes you made to the main document, and then turn off the preview.

Title	First Name	Last Name
Mr.	Sean	Corn
Mr.	Craig	Dostie
Ms.	Alexia	Lopez
Mr.	Winston	Boey
Ms	Phyllis	Cohen
Ms.	Margaret	Wong

26. Choose **Mailings→Finish→Finish & Merge** →**Edit Individual Documents**, and then click **OK** to merge all records.

27. Scroll through your letters, and then close the merged document without saving it.

28. Save and close the main document letter.

Merge Envelopes

29. Start a new blank document.

30. Choose **Mailings→Start Mail Merge→Start Mail Merge** →**Envelopes**.

31. Make sure the envelope is **Size 10** and click **OK**.
    Now you will attach the data source to your envelope.

32. Choose **Mailings→Start Mail Merge→Select Recipients** →**Use an Existing List**.

33. Navigate to your file storage location and open **WD07-R03-WalkerData-[FirstInitialLastName]**.

34. If necessary choose **Home→Paragraph→Show/Hide** ¶ to turn on formatting marks.

35. Type the following return address at the top paragraph symbol in the upper-left corner of the envelope:

```
Kids for Change
456 Bayside Road
Monterey CA 93943
```

36. Position the insertion point next to the paragraph symbol toward the middle of the envelope.

37. Choose **Mailings→Write & Insert Fields→Address Block** 🖹 , and then click **OK** to accept the default settings.

38. Choose **Mailings→Preview Results→Preview Results** 🔍 . Use the navigation buttons to view all envelopes then turn off the preview.

39. Choose **Mailings→Finish→Finish & Merge** 🖹→**Edit Individual Documents**, and then click **OK** to merge all records.

40. Scroll through the envelopes then close the file without saving it.

41. Save the envelope main document as `WD07-R03-WalkersEnv-[FirstInitialLastName]` in your **WD2013 Lesson 07** folder; close the document.
    Now you will merge the labels.

Generate Labels with Mail Merge

42. Start a new blank document.

43. Choose **Mailings→Start Mail Merge→Start Mail Merge→** 🖹 **Labels**.

44. Choose **Avery US Letter** as the Label Vendor and **5160 Easy Peel Address Labels** as the Product Number; click **OK**.

45. Choose **Mailings→Start Mail Merge→Select Recipients** 🖼→**Use an Existing List**.

46. Navigate to your **WD2013 Lesson 07** folder and open **WD07-R03-WalkerData-[FirstInitialLastName]**.

47. Ensure the insertion point is in the first label.

48. Choose **Mailings→Write & Insert Fields→Address Block** 🖹 and click **OK**.

49. Choose **Mailings→Write & Insert Fields→Update Labels** 🖹 to insert the Address Block code on all labels.

50. Choose **Mailings→Preview Results→Preview Results** 🔍 to see how the labels will look when they print, and then turn off the preview.
    Because the addresses are all three-line addresses, they fit on the label without removing Word's extra spacing.

51. Choose **Mailings→Finish→Finish & Merge** 🖹→**Edit Individual Documents**.

52. Click **OK** to merge all records, and then close the merged document without saving it.

53. Save the labels main document in your **WD2013 Lesson 07** folder as `WD07-R03-WalkerLabels-[FirstInitialLastName]`. Close the document and exit from **Word**.

54. Submit your final files based on the guidelines provided by your instructor.

Apply Your Skills

Create a Data Source and Main Document

In this exercise, you will create a data source, and then you will review the records and sort the list. Then you will specify a letter as a main document and insert merge fields in the letter.

Work with a Data Source

1. Start **Word**. Open **WD07-A01-SmallBiz** from your **WD2013 Lesson 07** folder and save it as `WD07-A01-SmallBiz-[FirstInitialLastName]`.

2. Specify the **SmallBiz letter** as the main document.
   Next you will customize the columns for your new data source.

3. Delete, add, and rename columns as needed to create the following fields in your data source:
   - Title
   - First Name
   - Last Name
   - Company Name
   - Address
   - City
   - State
   - Zip Code
   - Agent Name

4. Add the following records to your data source:

Mr. Tony Simpson Bigger Time Video Distributors 312 York Lane Richmond CA 94804 **Agent Name:** David Roth	Mr. Jason Jones Move It Distribution 2233 Crystal Street San Mateo CA 94403 **Agent Name:** Tammy Nelson	Ms. Debbie Thomas Barker Books 497 Tennessee Street Richmond CA 94804 **Agent Name:** Jacob Williams

5. Sort the data source in ascending alphabetic order by **Company Name**.

6. Save the data source as `WD07-A01-SmallBizData-[FirstInitialLastName]` in your **WD2013 Lesson 07** folder.

Work with the Main Document

7. In the main document, replace *INSIDE ADDRESS* with the **Address Block** code using the default formats.

8. Replace *GREETING LINE* with the **Greeting Line** code and change the ending punctuation to a colon.

9. In the last paragraph, replace *AGENT NAME* with the **Agent Name** code.

10. Preview the letters and check to be sure the spacing is correct.

11. Turn off the preview, and then make any needed changes to the main document.

12. Save and close the document; exit from **Word**.

13. Submit your final files based on the guidelines provided by your instructor.

    To view examples of how your file or files should look at the end of this exercise, go to the student resource center.

APPLY YOUR SKILLS WD07-A02

Merge Documents and Work with Merge Problems

In this exercise, you will merge letters, envelopes, and labels. You will also correct merge problems.

Conduct a Merge and Work with Merge Problems

1. Start **Word**. Open **WD07-A02-VisaLtr** from your **WD2013 Lesson 07** folder and save it as `WD07-A02-VisaLtr-[FirstInitialLastName]`.

2. Designate the letter as the main document.

3. Specify **WD07-A02-VisaData** in your **WD2013 Lesson 07** folder as the data source for this letter.

4. Preview the merge and notice that there are two errors in the greeting line.

5. Close the preview; edit the main document and preview the letters again, checking that the greeting line is correct.

6. Close the preview; save and close the main document.

Merge Envelopes and Labels

7. Start a new blank document and create a **Size 10** envelope as a main document with the following return address:

   ```
   Suzanne Frost
   Sales Manager
   Universal Corporate Events
   Middlefield CT 06455
   ```

8. Attach **WD07-A02-VisaData** as the data source for the envelope.

9. Insert an address block, using the default formats, in the middle of the envelope.

10. Preview the envelopes then close the preview.

11. Save the envelope main document as **WD07-A02-VisaEnv-[FirstInitialLastName]** in your **WD2013 Lesson 07** folder. Close the document.

12. Start a new blank document and create a labels main document using **Avery US Letter** as the Label Vendor and **5160 Easy Peel Address Labels** as the Product Number.

13. Attach **WD07-A02-VisaData** as the data source.

14. Insert the **Address Block** code in the first label using the default formats.

15. Use the **Update Labels** 🔃 command to replicate the Address Block code on all labels.

16. Preview the results and notice that the addresses don't fit well on the labels.

17. Close the preview, select the labels table, and remove Word's extra spacing in the Paragraph group on the Page Layout tab. Enter 0 in the Before field.

18. Preview the results again to ensure that the labels fit correctly.

19. Close the preview, and save the labels main document as **WD07-A02-VisaLabels-[FirstInitialLastName]** in your **WD2013 Lesson 07** folder.

20. Close the labels main document; exit from **Word**.

21. Submit your final files based on the guidelines provided by your instructor.

    To view examples of how your file or files should look at the end of this exercise, go to the student resource center.

APPLY YOUR SKILLS WD07-A03

Merge a Data Source and Main Documents, and Work with Merge Problems

In this exercise, you will create a data source using customized columns. You will add merge codes to main documents. You will preview and merge the main documents with the data source, make an editing change to a record, and sort the data source.

Work with a Data Source and Main Document

1. Start **Word**. Open **WD07-A03-TokyoLtr** from your **WD2013 Lesson 07** folder and save it as **WD07-A03-TokyoLtr-[FirstInitialLastName]**.

2. Specify the letter as the main document.

3. Start a new data source list.

4. Customize the columns by deleting and renaming fields. The final columns should be those shown here.
   - Title
   - First Name
   - Last Name
   - Company Name
   - Address
   - City
   - State
   - Zip Code

5. Create the data source shown here and save it as `WD07-A03-TokyoData-[FirstInitialLastName]` in your **WD2013 Lesson 07** folder.

Ms. Jasleen Mahal	Mr. George Iverson	Mr. Anthony Waldek
Superior Storage Devices	Superior Storage Devices	Superior Storage Devices
951 Industrial Way	951 Industrial Way	951 Industrial Way
Trenton NJ 08601	Trenton NJ 08601	Trenton NJ 08601

6. In the main document, replace *INSIDE ADDRESS* with the **Address Block** code using the default formats.

7. Replace *GREETING LINE* with the **Greeting Line** code using the default formats.

8. In the first paragraph, replace *COMPANY NAME* with the **Company Name** code.

9. In the last paragraph, replace *FIRST NAME* with the **First Name** code.

Preview the Results and Fix Merge Problems

10. Preview the merge and make sure the spacing is correct; close the preview.

11. Modify spacing in the main document if necessary.

    You've realized that the greeting line should be less formal, so you want to change the format to the recipient's first name.

12. Right-click the **Greeting Line** code, and choose **Edit Greeting Line** from the menu.

13. In the Greeting Line Format, click the drop-down arrow next to Mr. Randall, choose **Joshua** from the list, and click **OK**.

14. Preview the letters again to ensure the change was made.

15. Edit the recipient list, and change *Waldek* to **Waldecker**.

16. Sort the list in ascending alphabetic order by the **Last Name** column.

17. Merge the letter with the data source, choosing **Edit Individual Letters**, and then scroll through the letters.

18. Close the merged document without saving it; save and close the main document.

Merge Envelopes and Labels

19. Start a new blank document, designate it as a mail merge envelope, and use a **Size 10** envelope.

20. Insert the following return address on the envelope:

    ```
    Ms. Tasha Reynolds
    Universal Corporate Events
    456 Riverview Road
    Trenton NJ 08601
    ```

21. Attach the Tokyo data source to the envelope and insert the **Address Block** code.

22. Merge the envelopes and check them for accuracy.

23. If necessary, correct any errors and conduct the merge again.

24. Close the merged document without saving it; make any necessary changes.

25. Save the envelope main document as **WD07-A03-TokyoEnv-[FirstInitialLastName]** in your **WD2013 Lesson 07** folder. Close the document.

26. Start a new blank document and designate it as mail merge labels.

27. Choose **Avery US Letter** as the Label Vendor and **5160** as the Product Number.

28. Attach the Tokyo data source, insert the **Address Block** code in the first label, and update the labels to replicate the Address Block code in all.

29. Preview the labels and notice that the addresses don't fit well due to Word's extra spacing.

30. Close the preview, select the labels table, and remove the extra spacing.

31. Preview the labels again to verify the change in spacing; close the preview.

32. Save the labels main document as **WD07-A03-TokyoLabels-[FirstInitialLastName]** in your **WD2013 Lesson 07** folder. Close the document and exit from **Word**.

33. Submit your final files based on the guidelines provided by your instructor.

Extend Your Skills

In the course of working through the Extend Your Skills exercises, you will think critically as you use the skills taught in the lesson to complete the assigned projects. To evaluate your mastery and completion of the exercises, your instructor may use a rubric, with which more points are allotted according to performance characteristics. (The more you do, the more you earn!) Ask your instructor how your work will be evaluated.

WD07-E01 That's the Way I See It

You are planning a field trip for the fifth-grade class you teach. Create a two- to three-page permission letter informing parents of the trip and how it relates to students' school work (e.g., going to an aquarium after studying about ocean life). Ask parents to sign and then return the letter. Save the letter in your **WD2013 Lesson 07** folder as **WD07-E01-ParentLtr- [FirstInitialLastName]**.

Create a three-record data source of parent names and addresses and any other variables you choose. Customize the data source with only the column headings you need in the letter. Save the data source as **WD07-E01-ParentData-[FirstInitialLastName]**. Insert the merge field codes in the form letter and merge the main document and data source. Save the merged document as **WD07-E01-ParentLtrMerge-[FirstInitialLastName]**. Create an envelope main document with your return address, saved as **WD07-E01-ParentEnv- [FirstInitialLastName]**. Merge it with the data source. Save the merged document as **WD07-E01-ParentEnvMerge-[FirstInitialLastName]**.

You will be evaluated based on the inclusion of all elements specified, your ability to follow directions, your ability to apply newly learned skills to a real-world situation, your creativity, and the relevance of your topic and/or data choice(s). Submit your final files based on the guidelines provided by your instructor.

WD07-E02 Be Your Own Boss

You have created a rewards program for Blue Jean Landscaping customers. Create a form letter of two to three paragraphs describing how customers can accumulate points toward purchases. Mention three other benefits (make them up) for program members. Save the letter in your **WD2013 Lesson 07** folder as **WD07-E02-RewardsLtr-[FirstInitialLastName]**.

Create a data source of three customer's names and addresses and any other needed fields. Customize the data source for only those columns needed for the letter. Save the file as **WD07-E02-RewardsData-[FirstInitialLastName]**. Insert the merge field codes in the letter and conduct the merge, saving the merged document as **WD07-E02-RewardsMerge-[FirstInitialLastName]**.

You will include a brochure in the mailing, so use mailing labels for the oversized envelopes. Create a labels document named **WD07-E02-RewardsLabels-[FirstInitialLastName]** and merge it with your data source. Save the merged labels as **WD07-E02-MergeLabels-[FirstInitialLastName]**.

You will be evaluated based on the inclusion of all elements specified, your ability to follow directions, your ability to apply newly learned skills to a real-world situation, your creativity, and your demonstration of an entrepreneurial spirit. Submit your final files based on the guidelines provided by your instructor.

Transfer Your Skills

In the course of working through the Transfer Your Skills exercises, you will use critical-thinking and creativity skills to complete the assigned projects using skills taught in the lesson. To evaluate your mastery and completion of the exercises, your instructor may use a rubric, with which more points are allotted according to performance characteristics. (The more you do, the more you earn!) Ask your instructor how your work will be evaluated.

WD07-T01 Use the Web as a Learning Tool

Throughout this book, you will be provided with an opportunity to use the Internet as a learning tool by completing WebQuests. According to the original creators of WebQuests, as described on their website (WebQuest.org), a WebQuest is "an inquiry-oriented activity in which most or all of the information used by learners is drawn from the web." To complete the WebQuest projects in this book, navigate to the student resource center and choose the WebQuest for the lesson on which you are currently working. The subject of each WebQuest will be relevant to the material found in the lesson.

WebQuest Subject: How mail merge is used in business.

Submit your final file(s) based on the guidelines provided by your instructor.

WD07-T02 Demonstrate Proficiency

Stormy BBQ has added brisket of beef to its menu! They offered a free brisket of beef meal and a $20 gift certificate to the first five customers who visited their restaurant on New Year's Day. They plan to mail the certificates to the qualifying customers. As a Stormy BBQ employee, you have been asked to compose a congratulatory letter to go with the certificates. Since the letter will go to five people, it makes sense to use Word's Mail Merge feature.

Compose an appropriate letter with two or three paragraphs and save it as **WD07-T02-CertLtr-[FirstInitialLastName]** in your **WD2013 Lesson 07** folder. Create a name and address data source for the five winners. Customize the data source by adding any fields you want to use in your letter; delete any fields you don't intend to use. Save the data source as **WD07-T02-CertData-[FirstInitialLastName]**. Merge the letter and the data source and save the merged document as **WD07-T02-CertLtrMerge-[FirstInitialLastName]**.

Create an envelope main document to go with the mailing and include Stormy BBQ's return address and the Address Block code on a Size 10 envelope. Save the envelope main document as **WD07-T02-CertEnv-[FirstInitialLastName]**. Preview the envelopes and verify that they will print correctly.

Submit your final files based on the guidelines provided by your instructor.

WORD 2013

Creating a Newsletter

LEARNING OBJECTIVES

After studying this lesson, you will be able to:

- Insert section breaks
- Use WordArt and clip art
- Create and manipulate newsletter-style columns
- Use Building Blocks
- Apply Themes and Style Sets

In this lesson, you will use Word's Columns feature to create a newsletter. WordArt and clip art will add eye appeal to the newsletter. Using Building Blocks, design tools, and drop caps make creating professional-looking documents fast and easy. And, you will work with formatting tools to add special touches to your graphics. You will view your document in different modes, and you will change magnification with zoom controls.

Creating a Client Newsletter

Welcome to Green Clean, a janitorial product supplier and cleaning service contractor to small businesses, shopping plazas, and office buildings. Green Clean uses environmentally friendly cleaning products and incorporates sustainability practices wherever possible, including efficient energy and water use, recycling and waste reduction, and reduced petroleum use in vehicles. In addition to providing green cleaning services, the company also sells its eco-friendly products directly to customers.

You are an administrative assistant for Green Clean. It is nearing the beginning of a new quarter, and you are setting up the quarterly newsletter that will go to clients to keep them current on the happenings at your company. You will add pizzazz to the two-column newsletter by inserting WordArt and a picture, and by using the design tools to add color and other visual interest.

The Themes gallery provides a quick way to change overall document formatting.

These are examples of WordArt and a picture.

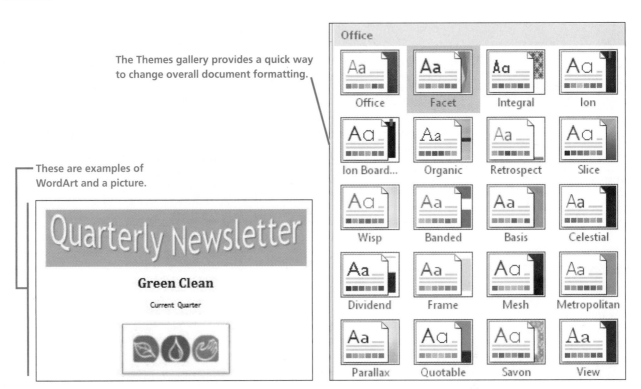

Working with Section Breaks

Video Library   http://labyrinthelab.com/videos   Video Number: WD13-V0801

In Word, whenever you make a document-level formatting change that doesn't apply to the whole document, you need one or more section breaks to define the portion of the document affected by the change. The example in this lesson is a columnar newsletter. The title lines at the top of the document are typed between the margins, which Word considers one column. Then the body of the newsletter is formatted in two columns. You need a section break to separate the one-column titles from the two-column body of the newsletter.

FROM THE RIBBON
Page Layout→Page
Setup→Breaks

Inserting Section Breaks

There are four types of section breaks, which are described in the following table.

Type of Section Break	Purpose
Next Page	Inserts a section break and starts the new section on the next page.
Continuous	Inserts a section break and starts the new section on the same page.
Odd Page	Inserts a section break and starts the new section on the next odd-numbered page; Word may insert a blank page to force the odd page section break.
Even Page	Inserts a section break and starts the new section on the next even-numbered page; Word may insert a blank page to force the even page section break.

The following illustration shows the use of continuous section breaks that are sectioning off the two-column portion of a document.

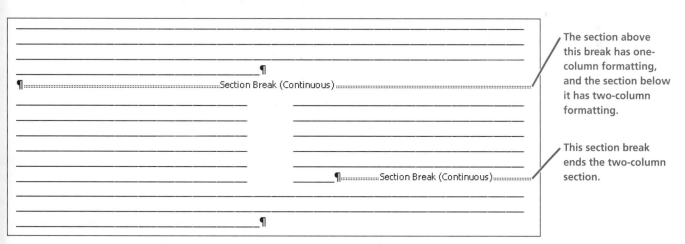

The section above this break has one-column formatting, and the section below it has two-column formatting.

This section break ends the two-column section.

DEVELOP YOUR SKILLS WD08-D01

Insert a Section Break

In this exercise, you will begin developing a newsletter by inserting three title lines and a section break.

1. If necessary, start a new document using the **Blank Document** template.

2. Choose **File→Save As** and save the document in your **WD2013 Lesson 08** folder as **WD08-D01-GreenClean-[FirstInitialLastName]**.

   Replace the bracketed text with your first initial and last name. For example, if your name is Bethany Smith, your filename would look like this: WD08-D01-GreenClean-BSmith.

3. If necessary, choose **Home→Paragraph→Show/Hide** ¶ to display formatting marks.

   You need to display formatting marks in order to see a section break.

4. If necessary, right-click the status bar and choose **Section** to display section numbers on the status bar.

5. Type these title lines at the top of the document:

   Quarterly Newsletter
   Green Clean
   Current Quarter

6. Tap Enter three times.

   Now you will insert a continuous section break.

7. Choose **Page Layout→Page Setup→Breaks** ⊟, and then choose **Continuous** from the menu.

   Now you can use document-level formatting above the break that is different from that below the break. Because formatting marks are turned on, you can see the section break.

8. Position the insertion point on the section break and tap Delete .

9. Click **Undo** ↻ to restore the section break.

10. Save the file and leave it open.

Using WordArt

Video Library   http://labyrinthelab.com/videos   Video Number: WD13-V0802

WordArt is great for creating smart-looking text objects. You can use the built-in designs as they are, or you can customize them. The following illustration displays the WordArt gallery.

FROM THE RIBBON
Insert→Text→Insert WordArt

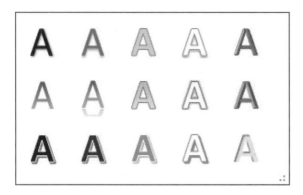

Selecting a WordArt Object

A WordArt object can have either a dotted-line or a solid-line border. When it's a dotted line, you can edit the text. Clicking on the dotted-line border changes it to a solid-line border. This means the entire object is selected, and you can change settings that affect everything within the WordArt object.

A dotted-line border indicates you can edit the text.

The solid-line border means you can change the object's settings.

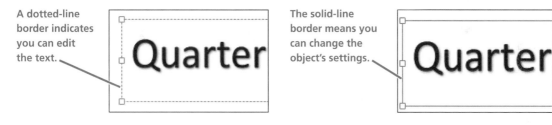

The terms *object* and *image* are both used when referring to graphical elements such as WordArt, clip art, and pictures.

Formatting WordArt

You edit and format a WordArt object using the tools located on the contextual Drawing Tools Format tab that appears when the object is selected. The small squares that surround a selected object are known as sizing handles. You can drag a handle to increase or decrease the size of the object. Sizing with a corner handle changes the length and width relative to their original proportions.

The rotation handle appears as a small circle with an arrowhead. You can drag the rotation handle left or right to rotate the object.

Mouse pointer as it appears on a WordArt sizing handle

Rotation handle

Layout Options

When an object is selected, a Layout Options smart tag appears to the right of the object. Clicking it displays six text-wrapping options that determine how the surrounding text behaves relative to the object, such as square, top and bottom, and behind text. If text is wrapped around an image and the image is selected, you'll see an anchor icon that indicates the image is attached to text.

FROM THE RIBBON
Picture Tools→
Format→Arrange→
Wrap Text

Anchor icon

Layout Options smart tag

Quarterly Newsletter

LAYOUT OPTIONS ✕

In Line with Text

With Text Wrapping

Text-wrapping options

Insert and Format a WordArt Object

In this exercise, you will use the newsletter title as the WordArt object. You will then wrap text around the WordArt object, change the background color, and add a text effect.

1. Save your file as **WD08-D02-GreenClean-[FirstInitialLastName]**.

2. Select *Quarterly Newsletter* in the first line but do not select the paragraph mark at the end of the line.

3. Choose **Insert→Text→Insert WordArt** 🄰, and then choose **Fill – Black, Text 1, Shadow** in the upper-left corner of the gallery.

   Notice the text is wrapped around the object. In this case, you don't want the text to wrap; you want it on its own line. You will fix this next.

4. With the WordArt object still selected, follow these steps to place it in line with text.

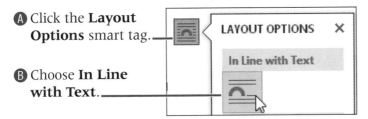

Ⓐ Click the **Layout Options** smart tag.

Ⓑ Choose **In Line with Text**.

5. Click in the document to close the smart tag, and then click the **WordArt object** to display its border.

The border appears as a dotted line.

6. Click the border to select the entire object.

The border now appears as a solid line. Next, you will change the background color.

7. Choose **Drawing Tools→Format→Shape Styles**.

8. Follow these steps to change the WordArt background color:

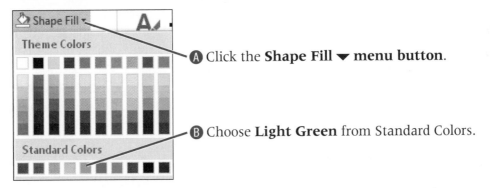

Ⓐ Click the **Shape Fill ▼ menu button**.

Ⓑ Choose **Light Green** from Standard Colors.

9. Choose **Drawing Tools→Format→WordArt Styles**.

10. Follow these steps to change the text color:

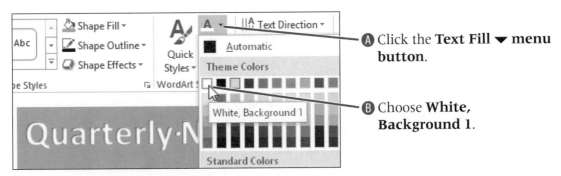

Ⓐ Click the **Text Fill ▼ menu button**.

Ⓑ Choose **White, Background 1**.

11. With the object still selected, choose **Drawing Tools→Format→WordArt Styles**.

12. Follow these steps to change the text effect:

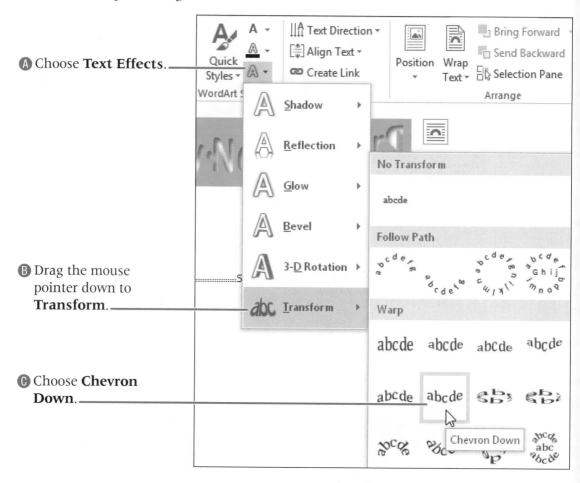

Ⓐ Choose **Text Effects**.

Ⓑ Drag the mouse pointer down to **Transform**.

Ⓒ Choose **Chevron Down**.

Format the Headings
Finally, you will center the headings and format the Green Clean heading.

13. Position the mouse pointer in the left margin area next to the WordArt object, and then click and drag down to select the object and the other two headings.

14. Choose **Home→Paragraph→Center** ☰.

15. Format *Green Clean* with the **Cambria, Bold, 18 pt** font.

    Compare your document headings with the following illustration.

16. Save your file.

Inserting Media, Pictures, and Clip Art

Video Library   http://labyrinthelab.com/videos   Video Number: WD13-V0803

Word offers a wide variety of graphic options you can use to liven up your documents, such as videos, pictures, and clip art. Word's graphic objects are easy to work with.

FROM THE RIBBON
Insert→Media→
Online Video

Adding Video to a Document

You can bring your documents to life by inserting online videos, which you can get from websites, blogs, and YouTube, for example. When you search and locate a video you think you might use, you can preview it online before inserting it in your document. Your readers can view the video from inside your document.

You can view the video in the search results screen before inserting it into your document.

Enhancing Your Documents with Pictures and Clip Art

You can browse through your computer or other computers to locate images for your document, or you can search online for images. The Microsoft website offers a variety of royalty-free pictures and clip art.

FROM THE RIBBON
Insert→Illustrations→
Pictures

Insert→Illustrations→
Online Pictures

You can search for pictures saved as files on a computer.

This command searches online for pictures and clip art.

A search on the
Microsoft website
for royalty-free
images.

Office.com Clip Art
8 search results for green clean

green clean

Sizing, Rotating, and Moving Images

Once you insert an image, you can change its size and degree of rotation. Like WordArt, clip art images and pictures have sizing handles and a rotation handle. When you hover the mouse pointer over a selected image, the four-headed move arrow appears. You must apply a text-wrapping option in order to freely move an image.

FROM THE RIBBON

Picture Tools→
Format→Size→Height
or Width to size an
image

The mouse pointer as it
appears on a sizing handle.

The mouse pointer as it appears
on the rotation handle.

You click and drag the four-
headed arrow to move an
object with a text-wrapping
option applied.

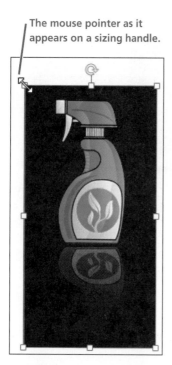

Cropping Images

Cropping allows you to hide parts of an image. You drag a cropping handle to hide the unwanted portion of the image. You can also un-crop an image. Cropping an image in Word does not affect the original image. The area hidden by cropping is not deleted. The mouse pointer appears as a T-shape when it's on a side, top, or bottom cropping handle. It appears as a right angle on a corner cropping handle.

FROM THE RIBBON

Picture Tools→
Format→Size→Crop
to crop an image

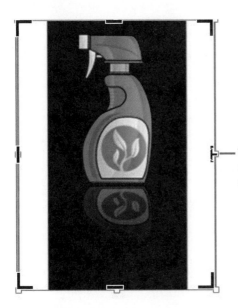

The mouse pointer appears on a side cropping handle as a sideways T-shape.

DEVELOP YOUR SKILLS WD08-D03

Insert, Crop, and Resize Clip Art

In this exercise, you will search for a clip art image online and place it in your document. You will crop the sides off the image as well as resize and move the image.

1. Save the file as **WD08-D03-GreenClean-[FirstInitialLastName]**.

2. Click the insertion point next to the paragraph symbol below the Current Quarter heading.

3. Choose **Insert→Illustrations→Online Pictures** to open the Insert Pictures search window.

4. Follow these steps to search for a piece of clip art:

Ⓐ Click in the search box, type **green clean**, and tap Enter.

Ⓑ Click this image. (If you can't locate this image, choose an appropriate "green clean" image.)

Ⓒ Click **Insert**.

The image appears at the insertion point. Now you will crop the white margins off the sides of the image. If you are using a different clip art image, practice the cropping steps for the experience.

5. Choose **Picture Tools→Format→Size→Crop** .

6. Follow these steps to crop the right-hand white margin off the picture:

Ⓐ Position the mouse pointer on the right-side cropping handle so it becomes a sideways T-shape.

Ⓑ Drag to the left until the mouse pointer touches the image's black background. (The cropped area turns gray as you drag.)

7. Repeat **step 6** to remove the white margin on the left side of the image.

8. Click in the document to hide the gray cropped areas, and then select the image again.
Now you will resize the image.

9. If necessary, choose **View→Show→Ruler** to display the ruler.

10. Follow these steps to resize the image:

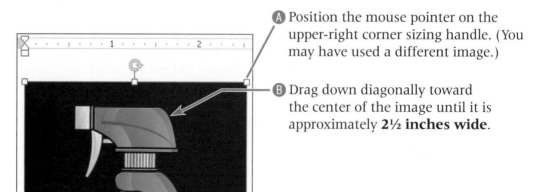

Ⓐ Position the mouse pointer on the upper-right corner sizing handle. (You may have used a different image.)

Ⓑ Drag down diagonally toward the center of the image until it is approximately **2½ inches wide**.

Now you will apply a text-wrapping option so you can drag the image to a new location.

11. With the image still selected, click the **Layout Options smart tag** to the right of the image and choose **Top and Bottom**. (Use ToolTips to locate the correct wrapping option.)

12. Drag the image to center it between the margins.

13. Save the file.

Formatting Images

Video Library   http://labyrinthelab.com/videos   Video Number: WD13-V0804

There are many tools on the contextual Format tab that allow you to customize images. For example, you can make blocks of color transparent, change the look of your image border, and apply different artistic effects.

FROM THE RIBBON
Picture Tools→
Format→Adjust→
Color

Setting a Transparent Color

Set Transparent Color is an option on the Color button menu. Images are made from tiny pixels of many different colors; that's what causes shade variation. When you click on a color in the object to make it transparent, all pixels of that same color are also made transparent.

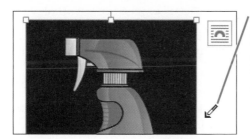

The mouse pointer changes to a pen when you choose Set Transparent Color.

The same image after the background is set to transparent.

Changing the Border Color

You can polish the look of an image with the Picture Border feature. It provides a wide variety of colors, weights, and line styles.

FROM THE RIBBON
Picture Tools→
Format→Picture
Styles→Picture Border

You can choose from theme colors, standard colors, and many additional colors.

The weight and line style are chosen here.

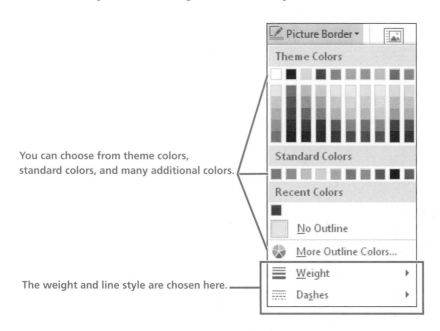

Applying Artistic Effects

You can take your image styling to the next level using special artistic effects. Some effects include a pencil sketch, line drawing, and painting. The following illustration displays the Pencil Sketch effect.

FROM THE RIBBON

Picture Tools→
Format→Adjust→
Artistic Effects

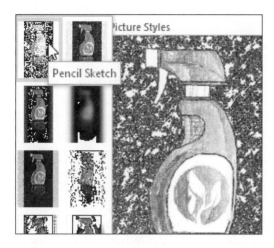

DEVELOP YOUR SKILLS WD08-D04
Format the Clip Art Image

In this exercise, you will remove the black background from the image and change the border. You will also experiment with artistic effects.

If you chose an image other than the one shown in this exercise, experiment with the features indicated but don't be concerned if your image doesn't behave exactly as the instructions indicate.

1. Save the file as **WD08-D04-GreenClean-[FirstInitialLastName]**.

2. If necessary, select the clip art image.

3. Choose **Picture Tools→Format→Adjust→Color** 🖼, and then choose **Set Transparent Color** at the bottom of the gallery.

   Notice when you move the mouse pointer onto the document, it appears as a pen.

4. Click in the black area on the clip art image.

   The background around the image should now be white, and all you see is a green bottle and its shadow. If you are using a different image, remember that Set Transparent makes all pixels of the same color transparent. If there are slight variations in shading, not all pixels will be transparent, which is fine for this exercise. Next you will crop the shadow from the image.

5. Choose **Picture Tools→Format→Size→Crop** 🖼, and then drag the bottom cropping handle up to the bottom of the bottle.

6. Click in the document to hide the gray cropped area, and then select the image again.

   Next you will format the picture border.

7. Choose **Picture Tools→Format→Picture Styles→Picture Border** 🖉.

8. Follow the steps to choose a line weight:

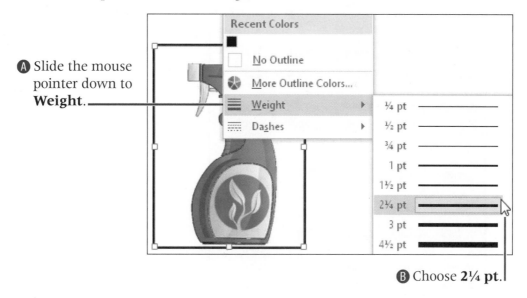

Ⓐ Slide the mouse pointer down to **Weight**.

Ⓑ Choose **2¼ pt**.

9. Choose **Picture Tools→Format→Picture Styles→Picture Border** 🖊, and then choose a border color that blends with the image.

Now you will experiment with artistic effects.

10. Choose **Picture Tools→Format→Adjust→Artistic Effects** 📇.

11. Slide the mouse pointer over several options to preview the effect on your image.

12. You won't apply an artistic effect, so click in the document to close the gallery.

13. Save the file.

Working with the Picture Styles Gallery

Video Library   http://labyrinthelab.com/videos   Video Number: WD13-V0805

Using the Picture Styles gallery is a quick way to enhance your images by adding frames, shadows, and directionality. The gallery uses live preview, allowing you to test various styles before deciding which one you want to apply.

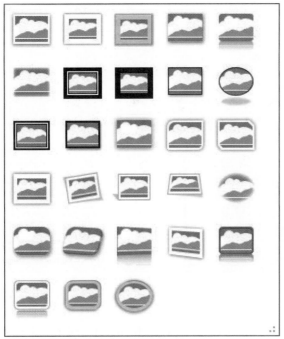

Picture Styles Gallery

Inserting a Picture from a File

In addition to being able to access pictures and clip art online, you can also insert pictures directly from files. For example, you can insert a scanned picture or a picture taken with a digital camera and stored on your computer.

Insert a Picture and Use Picture Styles

In this exercise, you will insert a picture from a file and apply a style from the Picture Styles gallery.

1. Save the file as **WD08-D05-GreenClean-[FirstInitialLastName]**.

2. Select the "green clean" clip art object you placed in the document and tap Delete .

3. If necessary, choose **Home→Paragraph→Show/Hide** ¶ to display formatting marks.

4. Position the insertion point on the blank line below the *Current Quarter* heading.

5. Choose **Insert→Illustrations→Pictures** .

6. Navigate to the **WD2013 Lesson 08** folder and double-click the **WD08-D05-GreenClean** picture file to insert it.

7. Crop the words *Green Clean* from the top of the picture, and then click in the document to hide the gray cropped area.

   Next you will right-align the picture to easily see the Picture Styles in Live Preview.

8. Select the picture and choose **Home→Paragraph→Align Right** .

9. Choose **Picture Tools→Format→Picture Styles**, and then click the **More** button to display the entire gallery.

10. Hover the mouse pointer over various options and observe the effect on the picture.

11. Choose the second option in the first row, **Beveled Matte, White**.

12. Choose **Home→Paragraph→Center** ▤.

13. Save the file.

Working with Newsletter-Style Columns

Video Library   http://labyrinthelab.com/videos   Video Number: WD13-V0806

You can use newsletter-style columns to arrange text in multiple columns. In a newsletter layout, text flows down one column and wraps to the top of the next column. Word automatically reformats column layout as you add or delete text.

FROM THE RIBBON
Page Layout→Page
Setup→Columns

Setting Up Columns

You can quickly set your text in columns with the Columns button on the Ribbon, or you can open the Columns dialog box where you can set up more sophisticated column layouts. For example, you can insert a line between columns and customize the width of each column.

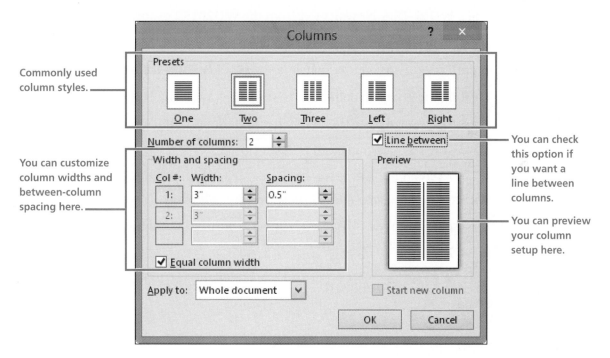

Commonly used column styles.

You can customize column widths and between-column spacing here.

You can check this option if you want a line between columns.

You can preview your column setup here.

Task	**Procedure**
Set up columns	■ Choose Page Layout→Page Setup→Columns and choose the desired number of columns; or, choose More Columns and enter the desired number of columns.
Insert a line between columns	■ Choose Page Layout→Page Setup→Columns→More Columns and check the Line Between checkbox.
Customize column widths	■ Choose Page Layout→Page Setup→Columns→More Columns and uncheck the Equal Column Width checkbox. ■ Use the spin box to change the size of column one; column two adjusts automatically.

DEVELOP YOUR SKILLS WD08-D06

Set Up Columns

In this exercise, you will open a document containing the content for your newsletter and copy it into the current document. Then you will format section two of your document with two columns, insert a line between the columns, and customize column widths.

1. Save the file as **WD08-D06-GreenClean-[FirstInitialLastName]**.

2. Open **WD08-D06-NewsltrTxt** from the **WD2013 Lesson 08** folder.

3. Press Ctrl + A to select the entire document.

4. Press Ctrl + C to copy the text, and then close **WD08-D06-NewsltrTxt**.

5. Position the insertion point next to the paragraph mark below the section break.

6. Press Ctrl + V to paste the newsletter text into your document.

7. Make sure the insertion point is in **section 2**.

8. Choose **Page Layout→Page Setup→Columns** ▤, and then choose **Two** from the menu.
   The text of the newsletter is now arranged in two columns.

9. Choose **Page Layout→Page Setup→Columns** ▤, and then choose **More Columns** from the menu to open the Columns dialog box.

10. Follow these steps to customize the columns:

Ⓐ Remove the checkmark from this checkbox.

Ⓑ Use the spin box to change the width of column 1 to **2"**.

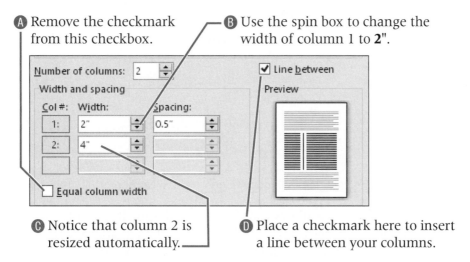

Ⓒ Notice that column 2 is resized automatically.

Ⓓ Place a checkmark here to insert a line between your columns.

11. Click **OK** and then scroll through the document to see the effect.

    The columns don't really look good this way. While you could Undo at this point, if you changed your mind at a later time, there is still a quick way to return the columns back to equal size.

12. Choose **Page Layout→Page Setup→Columns** 📑, and then choose **More Columns** to display the Columns dialog box.

13. Click the checkbox next to **Equal Column Width** and click **OK**.

14. Scroll through the document to see how it looks.

    It looks like it would be a good idea to balance the columns on the second page. You will do that in the next topic.

15. Save your file.

Working with Column Breaks

Video Library   http://labyrinthelab.com/videos   Video Number: WD13-V0807

You can manually force a column to end by inserting a column break, thus moving text at the break point to the top of the next column. This technique is often used to place headings at the top of columns and to balance columns on the last page of a multicolumn document.

FROM THE RIBBON

Page Layout→Page Setup→Breaks→ Column

Insert a Column Break

In this exercise, you will balance the second page of your newsletter by inserting a manual column break.

1. Save the file as **WD08-D07-GreenClean-[FirstInitialLastName]**.

2. Position the insertion point on **page 2**, at the beginning of the last paragraph in **column 1**. (The paragraph begins with *The Detergent metabolites….*)

3. Choose **Page Layout→Page Setup→Breaks→Column**.

4. If necessary, choose **Home→Paragraph→Show/Hide ¶** to display formatting marks. *Now you can see the column break.*

5. Choose **Home→Paragraph→Show/Hide ¶** to turn off formatting marks.

6. Save your file.

Using Building Blocks

Video Library   http://labyrinthelab.com/videos   Video Number: WD13-V0808

The Building Blocks feature allows you to insert predesigned content into your documents, including cover pages, headers and footers, watermarks, equations, and blocks of text. You can choose from the many built-in Building Blocks, or you can transform your own frequently used content into custom Building Blocks. Some Building Blocks appear in various galleries throughout the Ribbon, such as cover pages and page numbers. You can modify existing Building Blocks, delete custom Building Blocks, and sort the Building Block list in various ways.

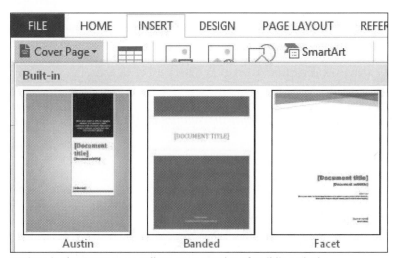

Designs in the Cover Page gallery are examples of Building Blocks.

QUICK REFERENCE	INSERTING BUILDING BLOCKS
Task	**Procedure**
Insert a Building Block	■ Type the Building Block name and tap F3; or, choose Insert→Text→Explore Quick Parts→Building Block Organizer, and then choose the desired entry.

Use a Built-In Building Block

In this exercise, you will add a cover page Building Block to your newsletter.

1. Save the file as **WD08-D08-GreenClean-[FirstInitialLastName]**.

2. Choose **Insert→Pages→Cover Page** 📄, scroll down, and choose **Semaphore**.
   A cover page is attached to the beginning of the document.

3. Click the **Document Title object** and type **Green Clean**.

   Now you will delete the unwanted text objects.

4. Click the **Document Subtitle object** and notice the tab labeled *Subtitle*.

5. Click directly on the **Subtitle tab**.
   This selects the entire object, not just the text.

6. Tap [Delete].
   Other text objects in the bottom-right corner are inside a graphic object frame. Rather than deleting the text objects individually, you can just delete the frame and the objects will be removed with it.

7. Follow these steps to remove unwanted objects:

   Ⓐ Click the insertion point next to the **Author object** to display the graphic object frame.

   Ⓑ Click the frame to select the entire object.

   AUTHOR
   [COMPANY NAME]
   [Company address]

   Ⓒ Tap [Delete].

8. Use the same technique to remove the **DATE object** at the top of the cover page. It is in a graphic object frame also.

9. Save your file.

Creating Custom Building Blocks

Video Library   http://labyrinthelab.com/videos   Video Number: WD13-V0809

You can create custom Building Blocks for content you use repeatedly. They can include a wide variety of items such as text, a clip art image, or a WordArt object. You can assign an item to the Quick Part gallery, or you can add it to an existing gallery, such as the Cover Page gallery.

Working with the Quick Part Gallery

The Quick Part gallery is a convenient location for storing custom Building Blocks.

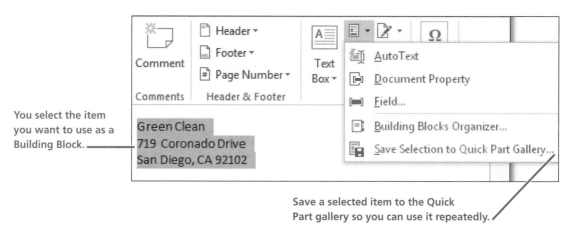

You select the item you want to use as a Building Block.

Save a selected item to the Quick Part gallery so you can use it repeatedly.

After you save a selection to the Quick Part gallery, you can reuse the selection by clicking Explore Quick Parts and choosing the selection from the gallery.

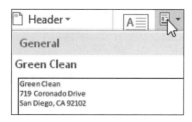

Modifying a Custom Building Block

There are two types of modifications to Building Blocks: changing the properties or modifying the actual content and formatting. If you want to change the name, gallery, where to save it, and so forth, you do so in the Modify Building Block dialog box. However, if you want to modify the actual content, you make the desired changes, select the content, and save the selection with the same name. Word will ask if you want to redefine the existing entry.

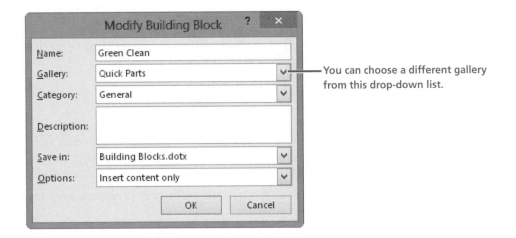

You can choose a different gallery from this drop-down list.

Create a Custom Building Block

In this exercise, you will type the contact information for the Green Clean company. You will then select it and save it to the Quick Part gallery.

1. Save the file as **WD08-D09-GreenClean-[FirstInitialLastName]**.

2. If necessary, choose **Home→Paragraph→Show/Hide** ¶ to turn on the formatting marks. Then, press Ctrl + End to move to the end of the document.

   It turns out that you can use some extra space at the bottom of the right-hand column, so you'll delete the column break.

3. Follow these steps to delete the column break:

   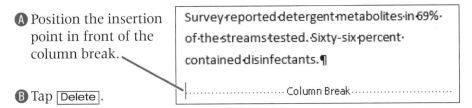

   A Position the insertion point in front of the column break.

   B Tap Delete.

4. Select the first paragraph symbol below the last paragraph in the right-hand column. (If necessary, tap Enter to generate a paragraph symbol.)

5. Choose **Home→Paragraph→Line and Paragraph Spacing** 🔁, and then choose **1.0** spacing.

6. Display the line spacing menu again, and this time, choose **Remove Space After Paragraph**.

7. Choose **Home→Paragraph→Show/Hide** ¶ to turn off formatting marks.

8. Type the following information:

   ```
   Green Clean
   719 Coronado Drive
   San Diego, CA 92102
   ```

9. Select the three lines that you just typed.

10. Choose **Insert→Text→Explore Quick Parts** 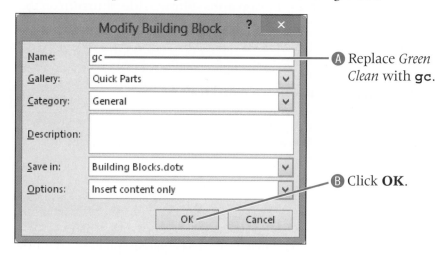→**Save Selection to Quick Part Gallery**.

11. When the Create New Building Block dialog box appears, click **OK**.

Insert the Custom Building Block

Now you will delete the address from the newsletter so you can test your new Building Block.

12. With the address still selected, tap [Delete].

13. If necessary, add a blank line at the bottom of the right-hand column, and position the insertion point on the blank line.

14. Choose **Insert→Text→Explore Quick Parts**, and then click your new **Building Block** at the top of the menu to insert it in the document.

Modify Building Block Properties

15. Choose **Insert→Text→Explore Quick Parts**.

16. Right-click the **Green Clean Building Block** at the top of the list and choose **Edit Properties** to open the Modify Building Block dialog box.

17. Follow these steps to change the name of the Building Block:

Ⓐ Replace *Green Clean* with **gc**.

Ⓑ Click **OK**.

18. Click **Yes** in the message box to redefine the entry.

Modify Building Block Contents

19. Position the insertion point at the end of the street address, tap [Spacebar], and type **Suite 200**.

20. Double-click the zip code and type **92108**.

21. Select the three-line name and address.

22. Choose **Insert→Text→Explore Quick Parts**, and then choose **Save Selection to Quick Part Gallery**.

23. Type **gc** for the Building Block name, and then click **OK**.

24. Click **Yes** in the message box to redefine the entry.

25. If necessary, select the three-line name and address at the bottom of the column; tap `Delete`.

26. Save your file.

Working with the Building Blocks Organizer

Video Library http://labyrinthelab.com/videos Video Number: WD13-V0810

The Building Blocks Organizer contains all Building Blocks, and you can manage them in the organizer. You can sort the list of Building Blocks in ascending order by clicking any of the column headings. You delete a Building Block through the organizer, and you can also insert and modify Building Block properties from within the organizer.

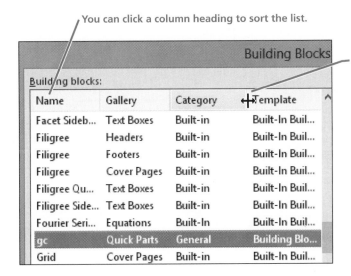

You can click a column heading to sort the list.

Positioning the mouse pointer between two column headings, then dragging left or right, narrows or widens the column.

QUICK REFERENCE	WORKING WITH CUSTOM BUILDING BLOCKS
Task	**Procedure**
Create a custom Building Block	▪ Select the content to convert to a Building Block, choose Insert→Text→Explore Quick Parts, and choose Save Selection to Quick Part Gallery. ▪ Make any desired changes in the Create New Building Block dialog box.
Delete a custom Building Block	▪ Choose Insert→Text→Explore Quick Parts→Building Blocks Organizer, select the Building Block, and click Delete. ▪ Open the gallery containing the Building Block to delete, right-click it, and choose Organize and Delete. ▪ With the Building Block highlighted, click Delete.
Sort the Building Block List	▪ Choose Insert→Text→Explore Quick Parts→Building Blocks Organizer and click any column header to sort in ascending order.

Delete a Custom Building Block

In this exercise, you will practice sorting the Building Blocks list. You will also delete a Building Block.

1. Save the file as **WD08-D10-GreenClean-[FirstInitialLastName]**.

2. Choose **Insert→Text→Explore Quick Parts** 📇.

3. Follow these steps to begin the deletion:

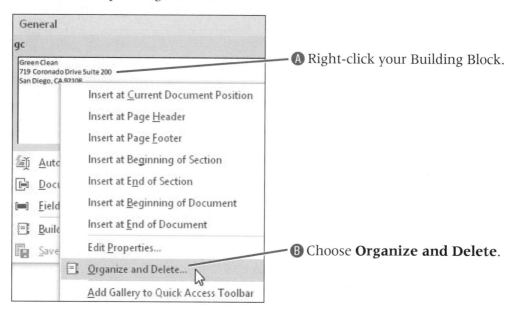

Ⓐ Right-click your Building Block.

Ⓑ Choose **Organize and Delete**.

Your gc Building Block is highlighted in the list.

4. Click **Delete** at the bottom of the dialog box.

5. When the message appears verifying the deletion, click **Yes**.

6. Click a few column headings to see the effect of column sorting, and then click the **Name** column heading to sort by the Name column.

7. Click **Close** at the bottom of the dialog box.

8. Save your file.

Working with Preformatted Text Boxes

Video Library   http://labyrinthelab.com/videos   Video Number: WD13-V0811

A preformatted text box is a box that you can type text in, and it's already formatted for you. Perhaps you have seen a quote in a magazine set in the middle or side of a page with some extra information the author wants to stand out from the rest of the article. These are referred to as pull quotes and sidebars. You can move and resize a text box. When you type in it, the text will wrap automatically. The preformatted text boxes are found in the Building Blocks Organizer.

QUICK REFERENCE	INSERTING A PREFORMATTED TEXT BOX
Task	**Procedure**
Insert a preformatted text box	■ Choose Insert→Text→Explore Quick Parts→Building Blocks Organizer, select the desired text box, and click Insert. ■ Type the text in the box, and then move or resize the box as desired.

Insert a Preformatted Text Box

In this exercise, you will insert a preformatted text box. You will then resize and move it. Finally, you will type a testimonial from a customer in it.

1. Save the file as **WD08-D11-GreenClean-[FirstInitialLastName]**.

2. If necessary, press Ctrl+End to move to the end of the document.

3. Choose **Insert→Text→Explore Quick Parts 📄→Building Blocks Organizer**.

4. Follow these steps to insert the Simple Quote text box:

Ⓐ If necessary, click **Name** to sort the list alphabetically.

Ⓑ Scroll down and choose **Simple Quote**.

Ⓒ Notice how the text box is formatted.

5. Click **Insert**.

   Don't worry about the text box location for the moment. You will enter text in the box, resize it, and then move it to a better location.

6. Type this text in the Simple Quote text box:

   We appreciate all you do for us and for our environment! Thank you for such excellent customer service. [Enter] **Daniels & Daniels, Inc.**

7. Drag to select the text. Then, using the Mini toolbar, change the **Font Size** to **10 pt**.

8. If necessary, choose **View→Show→Ruler** to turn it on.

9. Follow these steps to reduce the size of the text box:

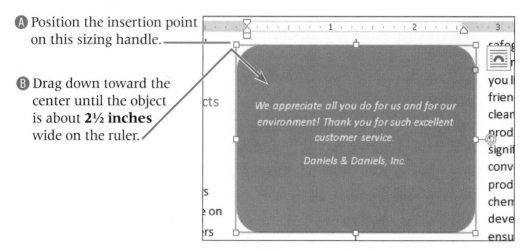

Ⓐ Position the insertion point on this sizing handle.

Ⓑ Drag down toward the center until the object is about **2½ inches** wide on the ruler.

10. With the text box selected, position the mouse pointer on the edge of the box so it becomes a four-headed arrow.

11. Drag the box around in the document and notice the square text wrapping.

    Live Layout lets you see how the text will look as you reposition it. In this example, you will place it at the bottom of the right-hand column on the last page.

12. Drag and drop the box down to the bottom of the column, as shown.

13. Save the file.

Using Themes and Style Sets

Video Library   http://labyrinthelab.com/videos   Video Number: WD13-V0812

Word has document-level formatting features that can instantly add color and visual variety to your entire document all at once. A Theme is a combination of colors, fonts, and graphic elements that you can apply to any document. Style Sets change font and paragraph properties. Style Sets create the biggest impact when you use Word's styles on the Home tab.

Themes and Style Sets appear next to each other on the Design tab, and they interact. That is, applying a Theme provides font and color schemes for the Style Sets. When you hover the mouse pointer over a Theme or Style Set, Live Preview displays the effect before you apply it.

Customizing a Theme

You can customize any Theme to match your creative side. You can change the colors, choose new fonts and paragraph spacing, and add effects to images, such as drawing shapes and SmartArt.

Changing Theme Colors

Built-in color schemes in a Theme are coordinated to work together. Changing a Theme color does not change the built-in Theme; it only modifies the colors in your current document. The colors not only affect the font color, but colors in objects, such as SmartArt and drawing shapes.

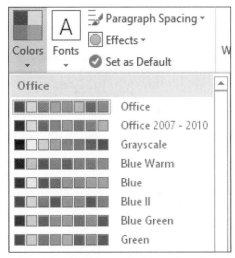

Each of these sets is a complete color scheme affecting text and fill colors.

Changing Theme Fonts

Themes use a set of coordinated fonts. Changing a Theme font changes any text formatted with fonts that have (Headings) or (Body) next to their names. Theme fonts may include the same font of different sizes or two different fonts that blend nicely.

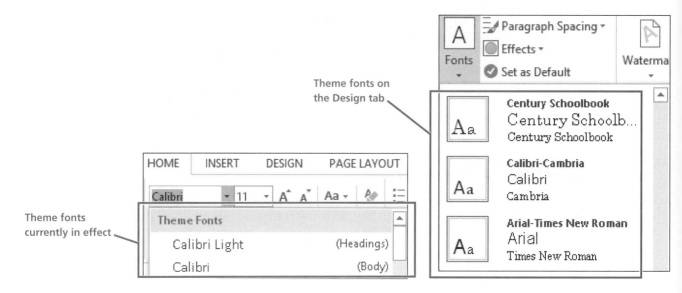

Theme fonts on the Design tab

Theme fonts currently in effect

DEVELOP YOUR SKILLS WD08-D12

Apply a Theme and Style Set to Your Newsletter

In this exercise, you will use Live Preview to examine a variety of Themes and Style Sets. You will also apply a new Theme and Style Set to your newsletter.

1. Save the file as **WD08-D12-GreenClean-[FirstInitialLastName]**.

2. Scroll up to the cover page and make sure the title is visible at the bottom of the page.
   The effect of Themes will be particularly easy to see on this page.

3. Choose **Design→Document Formatting→Themes** 🔲 to display the Themes gallery.

4. Hover the mouse pointer over several different **Themes** and observe the changes in your document.

5. Choose the **Facet Theme** (the second one in the first row).

6. Scroll through your document and see the impact of the new Theme.
   The headings in the body of the newsletter are formatted with Word's Heading 2 style; therefore, they respond to a change in the Theme. The text box has also taken on a new color from the Theme, and it has changed its position.

7. Drag the text box back to the bottom of the right-hand column.
   Next you will use Live Preview to see some of the color schemes.

8. Scroll to the last page and make sure the text box and a heading are visible.

9. Choose **Design→Document Formatting→Colors**  and slide the mouse pointer through the gallery to see the impact on the text box and titles.

10. Click in the document without choosing a new color.

   The green color scheme works well with the company name.

   Now you will use Live Preview to examine some of the Theme fonts.

11. Choose **Design→Document Formatting→Fonts** $\boxed{A}$, and then choose the Office font set (Calibri Light and Calibri) at the top of the menu.

Change the Style Set

12. Scroll in the document until one of the headings is positioned toward the bottom of the screen.

13. Choose **Design→Document Formatting**, and then click the **More** button on the Style Set gallery.

14. Follow these steps to apply a new Style Set:

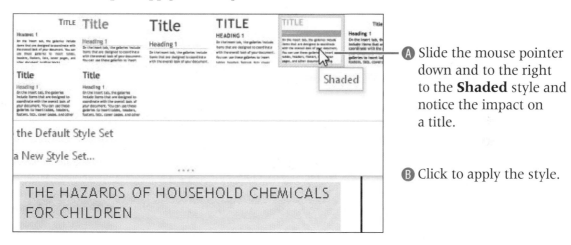

Ⓐ Slide the mouse pointer down and to the right to the **Shaded** style and notice the impact on a title.

Ⓑ Click to apply the style.

15. Save the file.

Inserting Drop Caps

Video Library   http://labyrinthelab.com/videos   Video Number: WD13-V0813

A drop cap is a large uppercase first letter of a paragraph. You have the option of leaving it in the paragraph itself with the text wrapped around it or placing it in the margin next to the paragraph. Other options include changing the font for the drop cap, modifying the number of lines to drop, and setting the distance from the other text.

FROM THE RIBBON
Insert→Text→Add a Drop Cap

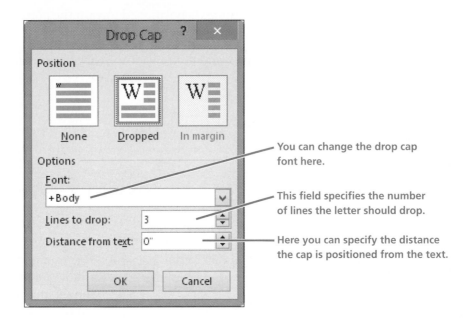

You can change the drop cap font here.

This field specifies the number of lines the letter should drop.

Here you can specify the distance the cap is positioned from the text.

Drop cap in the paragraph with text wrapping.

> We have exciting news to share! After experiencing much success in the Richmond area, Green Clean is expanding into the Charlottesville area. The

Drop cap in the margin.

> We have exciting news to share! After experiencing much success in the Richmond area, Green Clean is expanding into the Charlottesville area. The expansion will include

DEVELOP YOUR SKILLS WD08-D13

Insert a Drop Cap

In this exercise, you will insert a drop cap in the newsletter.

1. Save the file as **WD08-D13-GreenClean-[FirstInitialLastName]**.

2. Scroll to **page 2** and select the *W* in the word *We* in the first column.

3. Choose **Insert→Text→Add a Drop Cap** ▣→**Dropped**, and then click in the document to deselect the drop cap.

4. Save the file.

WHAT'S NEW?

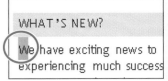

Working with Views

Video Library   http://labyrinthelab.com/videos   Video Number: WD13-V0814

Word lets you view your document in several ways. Each view is optimized for specific types of work. The views change the way documents appear on the screen but have no impact on the appearance of printed documents. You can choose views from the View tab or the status bar.

Views on the View tab

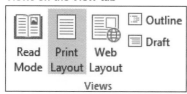

Views on the status bar

DOCUMENT VIEWS	
View	**Description**
Read Mode	This view provides a book-like reading experience with pages laid out side by side. The Ribbon disappears to display more of your document. You navigate horizontally, as in a book.
Print Layout	With this default view, your documents look similar to the way they will look when printed. You can see graphics, headers and footers, and multi-column layouts.
Web Layout	This view displays your document as it would look as a web page. It appears as one long page without page breaks.
Outline	Outline view is useful for organizing long documents.
Draft	This view simplifies page layout by eliminating elements, such as headers and footers and graphic elements. This view is useful when you want to focus on content.

DEVELOP YOUR SKILLS WD08-D14
Change the View

In this exercise, you will try out various views.

1. Position the insertion point at the top of the document.

2. Locate the **View** buttons at the right end of the status bar.

3. Click the first button, **Read Mode** ▓, and notice how the look of your newsletter has changed.

4. Click the arrow at the right side of the window to scroll through the document.

5. Click the third button, **Web Layout** ▓, and scroll through the document. Notice that it displays as one long page, like a web page.

   Now you'll try a few more views.

6. Choose **View→Views→Outline** 🔲.

   Outline view lets you see your document sections in a hierarchical fashion, which helps you see the overall flow of your document. It is probably not the best view for a document laid out as a newsletter.

7. Choose **View→Views→Draft** 🔲.

   Draft view simplifies the document's layout, so you can focus on content.

8. Finally, choose **View→Views→Print Layout** 🔲.

Using Zoom Controls

Video Library   http://labyrinthelab.com/videos   Video Number: WD13-V0815

The Zoom commands on the View tab let you change the magnification of your document and control the number of pages you can display at one time.

The Zoom button opens the Zoom dialog box.

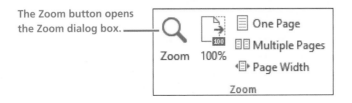

You can customize the percent of magnification here.

Dragging over the Many Pages grid allows you to choose many pages at once. (The grid expands if you click and continue to drag.)

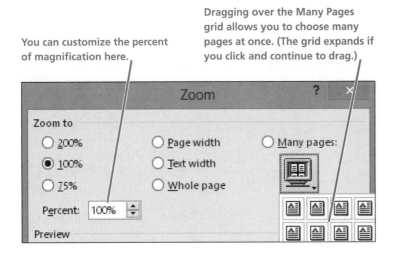

The Zoom bar in the bottom-right corner of the Word window provides a quick way to change magnification.

You can click the Zoom Out and Zoom In buttons to change magnification.

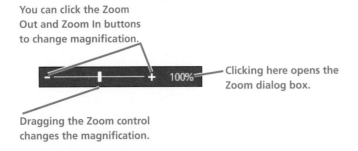

Clicking here opens the Zoom dialog box.

Dragging the Zoom control changes the magnification.

Use the Zoom Controls

In this exercise, you will use your newsletter to practice with the Zoom controls.

1. Position the insertion point at the top of the page following the cover page.

2. Choose **View→Zoom→Zoom** 🔍 to open the Zoom dialog box.

3. Follow these steps to display all pages at once:

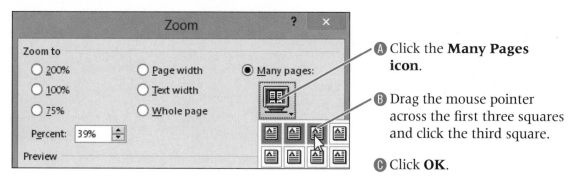

Ⓐ Click the **Many Pages icon**.

Ⓑ Drag the mouse pointer across the first three squares and click the third square.

Ⓒ Click **OK**.

The way the pages are laid out on the screen depends on the size of your screen.

4. Click the **Zoom In** button on the status bar enough times to return to **100%** magnification.

5. Right-click the status bar and choose **Section** to remove the *Section* indicator from the status bar.

6. Save and close the file. Exit **Word**. (If you are prompted to save changes to Building Blocks, click **Don't Save**.)

Concepts Review

To check your knowledge of the key concepts introduced in this lesson, complete the Concepts Review quiz by choosing the appropriate access option below.

If you are...	Then access the quiz by...
Using the Labyrinth Video Library	Going to http://labyrinthelab.com/videos
Using eLab	Logging in, choosing Content, and navigating to the Concepts Review quiz for this lesson
Not using the Labyrinth Video Library or eLab	Going to the student resource center for this book

Reinforce Your Skills

Insert Section Breaks, Graphics, and Newsletter Columns

In this exercise, you will create a newsletter with section breaks and columns, and you will insert and work with graphic images.

Work with Section Breaks

1. Start **Word**. Create a new document using the **Single Spaced (Blank)** template, and save it in your **WD2013 Lesson 08** folder as `WD08-R01-SchoolHabitat-[FirstInitialLastName]`.

2. If necessary, choose **Home→Paragraph→Show/Hide** ¶ to display formatting characters.

3. If necessary, right-click the status bar and choose **Section**.

4. Type these lines at the top of the document:

   `Schoolyard Habitat`
   `Kids for Change`

5. Tap Enter three times.

6. Choose **Page Layout→Page Setup→Breaks→ Continuous**.

Insert WordArt

7. Select the *Schoolyard Habitat* heading but not the paragraph mark at the end of the line.

8. Choose **Insert→Text→WordArt** 𝐴, and then choose **Fill – Blue, Accent 1, Shadow**.
   Next you will use the Layout Options smart tag to position the second line below the WordArt image.

9. With the WordArt object selected, click the smart tag and choose **In Line with Text**.

10. If necessary, click the dotted line border of the image to select the entire image.

11. Choose **Drawing Tools→Format→Word Art Styles→Text Effects** 𝐴, and then slide the mouse pointer down to **Glow**.

12. In the Glow Variations section, choose **Green, 11 Pt Glow, Accent Color 6**.

13. Choose **Drawing Tools→Format→Word Art Styles→Text Fill ▼ menu button**.

14. Choose the fifth color in the last column, **Green, Accent 6, Darker 25%**.

15. Position the mouse pointer in the margin area to the left of the WordArt image, and drag down to select it and the *Kids for Change* line.

16. Choose **Home→Paragraph→Center** ≡.

17. Format *Kids for Change* with **Comic Sans MS**, **Bold**, **16 pt** font.

18. Position the insertion point on the paragraph symbol below the section break.

19. Choose **Insert→Text→Object ▾ menu button** and choose **Text from File**.

20. Navigate to your **WD2013 Lesson 08** folder and insert **WD08-R01-HabitatContent**.

21. Position the insertion point on the second blank line below the text you just inserted.

22. Choose **Page Layout→Page Setup→Breaks ⊟→Continuous**.

23. Position the insertion point on the second blank line below the second section break.

Insert, Size, and Format a Picture

24. If necessary, choose **View→Show→Ruler** to display the ruler.

25. Choose **Insert→Illustrations→Online Pictures** 🖼️.

26. Type **butterfly** in the search box and tap Enter.

27. Choose the picture shown and click **Insert**. (If you can't locate this picture, choose a similar one.)

28. If necessary, click the picture to select it. Then, position the mouse pointer on the upper-right corner sizing handle.

29. When the mouse pointer appears as a double-headed arrow, drag down toward the middle of the picture until it's approximately **3½ inches wide**.

30. Make sure the picture is still selected.

31. Choose **Picture Tools→Format→Picture Styles**, and then click the **More ▾** button at the bottom-right corner of the Picture Styles gallery.

32. Choose the last picture style in the fourth row, **Soft Edge Oval**.

33. Choose **Home→Paragraph→Center** 🗏.

Apply Columns

34. Position the insertion point in **section 2**.

35. Choose **Page Layout→Page Setup→Columns ▤→More Columns**.

36. Choose **Two** in the Presets area. Also click to place a checkmark in the **Line Between** checkbox.

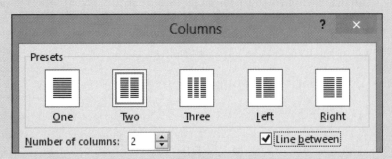

37. Click **OK**.

The Habitat Team *heading should be moved to the top of the second column.*

38. Position the insertion point in front of the heading at the bottom of the first column.

39. Choose **Page Layout→Page Setup→Breaks ▤→Column**.

40. Choose **File→Print** to preview the document.

41. Click the **Back** ◉ button in the upper-left corner of the Print window.

42. Right-click the status bar and choose **Section** to turn off the Section indicator on the status bar, and then click in the document to close the menu.

43. Save and close the file; exit **Word**.

44. Submit your final file based on the guidelines provided by your instructor.

To see examples of how your file or files should look at the end of this exercise, go to the student resource center.

REINFORCE YOUR SKILLS WD08-R02

Use Building Blocks, Themes, Style Sets, and Drop Caps

In this exercise, you will insert a built-in Building Block and create a custom Building Block. You will apply a Theme and Style Set to a document, and insert a drop cap. Finally, you will work with views and zoom controls.

Insert a Building Block

Roger Washington, a member of Kids for Change, has written a report on wetlands to present at the next monthly meeting. He has prepared a handout, and now he will add polish to the document.

1. Start **Word**. Open **WD08-R02-Wetlands** from the **WD2013 Lesson 08** folder and save it as `WD08-R02-Wetlands-[FirstInitialLastName]`.

To begin, you will add a cover page Building Block.

2. Choose **Insert→Pages→Cover Page** 📄, and then scroll down and choose **Whisp**.

3. Click the **Document Title** object and type `Wetlands`.

4. Click the **Document Subtitle** object and type `Why They Are Important`.

5. Scroll to the bottom of the cover page, click the **Author Name** object, and type `Roger Washington`.

6. Click the **Company Name** object, click directly on the **Company tab**, and tap `Delete`.

7. Use the same technique to delete the **Date** text object at the top of the cover page.

8. If necessary, choose **Home→Paragraph→Show/Hide** ¶ to display formatting marks.

9. Scroll to **page 2** and position the insertion point on the second blank line below the last paragraph.

10. Type this text: `If you want to be part of the wetlands project, please contact me.`

Create a Custom Building Block

11. Position the insertion point on the second blank line below the line you just typed.

12. Type this contact information:

```
Roger Washington
415-555-1234
Roger@Yahoo.com
```

13. Select the three lines you just typed.

14. Choose **Insert→Text→Explore Quick Parts** 📄**→Save Selection to Quick Part Gallery**.

15. When the Create New Building Block dialog box opens, click **OK**.
    Now you will test your Building Block.

16. With the contact information still selected, tap `Delete`.

17. Choose **Insert→Text→Explore Quick Parts** 📄, and then click your custom **Building Block** at the top of the menu.

Modify Building Block Properties

18. Choose **Insert→Text→Explore Quick Parts** 📄.

19. Right-click your **Building Block** and choose **Edit Properties**.

20. Change the name of the Building Block to `rw` as shown.

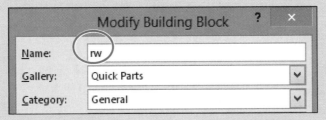

21. Click **OK**. Then, click **Yes** to redefine the entry.

22. Position the insertion point between Roger and the "at sign" (@) in the email address and type **qw**.

23. Select the three lines of contact information.

24. Choose **Insert→Text→Explore Quick Parts** 📧**→Save Selection to Quick Part Gallery**.

25. Type **rw** for the name and click **OK**.

26. Click **Yes** to redefine the entry.

Delete a Building Block from the Organizer

27. Choose **Insert→Text→Explore Quick Parts** 📧.

28. Right-click your **Building Block** and choose **Organize and Delete**.
    Your Building Block is highlighted in the list.

29. Click **Delete** at the bottom of the dialog box, and then click **Yes** to verify the deletion.

30. Close the **Building Blocks Organizer**.

Use a Theme and a Style Set

31. Choose **Design→Document Formatting→Themes** 🅰, and then choose the last Theme in the second row, **Slice**. Scroll through the document to see the impact of the new Theme.

32. Choose **Design→Document Formatting**, and then click the **More** ⏷ button.

33. Choose the first Style Set in the Built-In category, **Basic (Elegant)**.
    Notice that the new Style Set changed the spacing. Next, you will tighten up the spacing in the contact information.

34. Scroll to the bottom of **page 2** and select the three contact lines at the bottom of page 2 and the top of page 3.

35. Choose **Home→Paragraph→Line and Paragraph Spacing** 📑**→Remove Space After Paragraph**.

36. Delete the paragraph symbol above Roger Washington's name.

37. Position the insertion point at the end of Roger's email address and tap Delete to remove the blank page at the end of the document.

Insert a Drop Cap

38. Scroll to the top of **page 2** and select the *W* at the beginning of the first paragraph.

39. Choose **Insert→Text→Add a Drop Cap** ⎍**→Dropped**.

40. Choose **Home→Paragraph→Show/Hide** ¶ to turn off formatting marks.

Work with Views

41. Press ⎘Ctrl⎙ + ⎘Home⎙.

42. Choose **View→Views→Read Mode** ⎗.

43. Click the arrow on the right side of the window to see the rest of the document.

44. Click the **Print Layout** ⎘ button at the right side of the status bar.

45. Choose **View→Views→Draft** ⎘. Then, scroll through the document and notice that the graphic elements are suppressed.

46. Choose **View→Views→Print Layout** ⎘.

Use Zoom Controls

47. Choose **View→Zoom→Zoom** ⎘.

48. In the Zoom dialog box, click the **Many Pages** icon.

49. Drag the mouse pointer across the first two squares, click the second square, and click **OK**.
Notice the setting of the Zoom bar at the right edge of the status bar.

50. Click the **Zoom In** button enough times to return the magnification to **100%**.

51. Save and close the file. (If you see a message prompting you to save changes to Building Blocks, click **Don't Save**.) Exit **Word**.

52. Submit your final file based on the guidelines provided by your instructor.
To see examples of how your file or files should look at the end of this exercise, go to the student resource center.

Create a Newsletter

In this exercise, you will create a newsletter using a section break, columns, WordArt, and a picture. You will insert Building Blocks and create a custom Building Block. You will also apply a Theme and a Style Set, and add a drop cap. Finally, you will work with views and zoom controls.

Work with Section Breaks

1. Start **Word**. Open **WD08-R03-WaterPollution** from your **WD2013 Lesson 08** folder and save it as `WD08-R03-WaterPollution-[FirstInitialLastName]`.

2. If necessary, right-click the status bar and choose **Section** to display section numbers on the status bar. Then click in the document to close the menu.

3. If necessary, choose **Home→Paragraph→Show/Hide** ¶ to display formatting marks.

4. Position the insertion point on the second paragraph symbol below the heading at the top of the document.

5. Choose **Page Layout→Page Setup→Breaks** ⊟ **→Continuous**.

Use Word Art

6. Select the heading at the top of the document but not the paragraph symbol at the end of the line.

7. Choose **Insert→Text→Insert WordArt** ⎐, and then choose **Fill – Blue, Accent 1, Outline – Background 1, Hard Shadow – Accent 1**.

8. With the WordArt object selected, click the **Layout Options smart tag**.

9. Choose the **Top and Bottom** layout.

10. Choose **Drawing Tools→Format→WordArt Styles→Text Effects** Ⓐ and slide the mouse pointer down to **Transform**.

11. Choose **Square** in the **Warp** category.

12. Position the insertion point on the **WordArt border** and drag to the right to center the object between the margins.

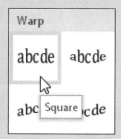

13. Position the insertion point on the second blank line below the last paragraph.

Insert and Format a Picture

14. Choose **Insert→Illustrations→Online Pictures** ⊞.

15. Type **fishing** in the search box and tap ⌷Enter⌷.

16. Scroll down the gallery about a third of the way and click the image shown here. (If you can't find this one, choose any other.)

17. Click **Insert**.

18. If necessary, choose **View→Show→Ruler** to turn on the ruler.

19. Position the mouse pointer on the upper-right sizing handle, and then drag until the picture is about three inches wide.

20. Choose **Picture Tools→Format→Size→Crop** 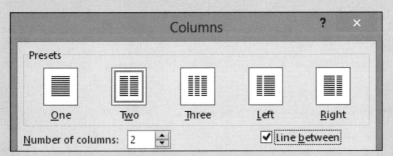.

21. Position the mouse pointer on the cropping handle on the left side of the picture, and then drag to the right about a half inch. (If you are using a different picture, just crop the picture for the experience.)

22. Click in the document to hide the cropped area, and then select the picture again.

23. Choose **Picture Tools→Format→Picture Styles**, and then click the **More** button on the bottom-right corner of the Picture Styles gallery.

24. Choose the first style in the second row, **Soft Edge Rectangle**.

Work with Columns

25. Position the insertion point in the body text.

26. Choose **Page Layout→Page Setup→Columns** →**More Columns**.

27. In the Columns dialog box, choose **Two** in the Presets section and click to add a checkmark in the **Line Between** checkbox.

28. Click **OK**.

The tops of the columns are not even, so you'll fix that now.

29. Delete the paragraph symbol above the **Tim Johnson** paragraph.

Now you'll insert a column break so the two lines at the bottom of the left column will float to the top of the second column.

30. Position the insertion point before the first line of the bottom paragraph in the left column.

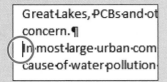

31. Choose **Page Layout→Page Setup→Breaks** →**Column**.

Use Building Blocks

32. Position the insertion point on the blank line below the picture in the right-hand column.

33. Choose **Insert→Text→Explore Quick Parts→▣→Building Blocks Organizer**.

34. If necessary, click the **Name** column header to sort the list by name.

35. Choose **Austin Quote** and click **Insert**.

    Don't be concerned about the position of the text box. You'll fix that shortly.

36. Click the dotted line border to make it solid, thus selecting the entire object.

37. Choose **Home→Font** and choose **9 point** as the font size.

38. Click the default text to select it, and then type this text:

    `If you can volunteer for the Waterways Tour, please contact me at Timj@Yahoo.com.`

    Now you'll resize the text box so it will fit in the right-hand column.

39. Position the mouse pointer on the right-side sizing handle and drag left until the word *Tour* is at the end of the first line.

40. Position the mouse pointer on the border of the text box, and then drag up and to the right until the text box is below the picture in the right-hand column. (It may be necessary to resize the picture to make room for the quote box.)

    Now you'll create a custom Building Block.

41. Position the insertion point at the end of the first paragraph in the left column and tap Enter.

42. Type **Think globally, act locally!**

43. Select the line but not the paragraph symbol at the end of the line.

44. Choose **Insert→Text→Explore Quick Parts ▣→Save Selection to Quick Part Gallery**.

45. When the Create New Building Block dialog box opens, type **tg** as the name, and click **OK**.

46. Delete the selected text in the document so you can test your Building Block.

47. Choose **Insert→Text→Explore Quick Parts ▣**, and then click your **Building Block** at the top of the menu.

    Now you'll delete the Building Block so the next student who uses your computer will have the same experience.

48. Choose **Insert→Text→Explore Quick Parts ▣**, right-click your **Building Block**, and choose **Organize and Delete**.

    Your Building Block is selected in the list.

49. Click **Delete**, and then click **Yes** to verify the deletion.

50. Close the **Building Blocks Organizer**.

Use Themes and Style Sets

51. If necessary, scroll up so you can see the WordArt.

52. Choose **Design→Document Formatting→Themes**, and then choose **Frame**.

Notice the impact on the WordArt, the headings within the document, and the text box. There has also been a font change.

53. Choose **Design→Document Formatting**, click the **More** button in the Style Set gallery, and choose **Basic (Simple)**.

Insert a Drop Cap

54. Select the *T* at the beginning of the first paragraph.

55. Choose **Insert→Text→Add a Drop Cap**→**Dropped**.

56. Click in the body of the document to deselect the drop cap.

57. Choose **Home→Paragraph→Show/Hide** ¶ to turn off formatting marks.

Work with Views

58. Click the **Web Layout** button at the right side of the status bar and notice the change to the document.

59. Choose **View→Views→Outline** and notice how the view changes.

60. Click the **Print Layout** button on the status bar.

Use Zoom Controls

61. Drag the **Zoom** button on the Zoom bar to the left and right to see the effect, and then set the zoom at **75%**.

62. Choose **View→Zoom→100%**.

63. Save and close the document; exit **Word**. (If you are prompted to save changes to Building Blocks, click **Don't Save**.)

64. Submit your final file based on the guidelines provided by your instructor.

Apply Your Skills

Use Section Breaks, Graphic Images, and Columns

In this exercise, you will create a newsletter with section breaks, columns, and graphic images.

Work with Section Breaks and Use WordArt

1. Start **Word**. Open **WD08-A01-CorpTravel** from your **WD2013 Lesson 08** folder and save it as **WD08-A01-CorpTravel-[FirstInitialLastName]**.

2. If necessary, choose **Home→Paragraph→Show/Hide ¶** to display formatting marks.

3. Position the insertion point on the second blank line below the two heading lines at the top of the document and insert a **continuous section break**.

4. Apply **WordArt** to the first line heading using the last style in the second row, **Fill – Gray-50%, Accent 3, Sharp Bevel**.

5. Use the **Layout Options** smart tag to apply **Top and Bottom** text wrapping.

6. Apply the **Can Up** text effect in the Transform category to the WordArt object.

7. Choose **Drawing Tools→Format→Text Fill** **A**, and then choose **Blue, Accent 5, Lighter 40%**.

8. Format the second heading line, *Meeting and Event Planning Services*, with **Tahoma 14 pt font**.

9. Center both heading lines. (You have to drag the WordArt object to center it.)

10. Position the insertion point at the beginning of the first subheading.

> Dear·Corporate·Travel·Agent,¶
>
> This·month's·newsletter·focuses·on
> focuses·on·Starwood·Hotels·&·Reso
> interview·with·Jet·Blue's·Dennis·Co
>
> ▪ Starwood·Corporate·Rate
> February·07,·2013--·01:05·PM·ET¶

11. Tap Enter and then position the insertion point on the blank line.

Insert and Format Clip Art

12. Choose **Insert→Illustrations→Online Pictures** 🖼. Search for `hotel`.

13. Insert the image shown. (If you can't locate the image, choose a similar one. The image should be approximately 2″ wide and 1 1/2″ high. If you chose a different image, you may need to resize it.)

14. Add the **White, Background 1, Darker 25%** picture border around the picture.

15. Apply **3 pt line weight** to the border.

16. Use the **Layout Options** smart tag to apply the **Top and Bottom** layout to the clip art.

17. Position the insertion point in front of the second subheading (on page 2).

18. Tap ⌷Enter⌷ and then position the insertion point on the blank line.

19. Use the **Online Pictures** 🖼 feature and the Office.com Clip Art search box to search for `airplane`.

20. Insert the image shown (or a similar one).

21. Resize the image to approximately **2 inches** wide.

22. Place the same border color around the image as that used for the hotel image, and use a **3-pt line weight**.

23. Position the insertion point on the blank line at the end of the document and type this text: **Thanks to our loyal Universal Corporate Events clients!**

24. Tap [Enter].

25. Format the line you just typed with **Bold 14 pt**. Then, position the insertion point on the blank line below that line.

26. Use the **Online Pictures** feature and the **Office.com Clip Art search box** to search for **`travel`**.

27. Insert the image shown (or a similar one).

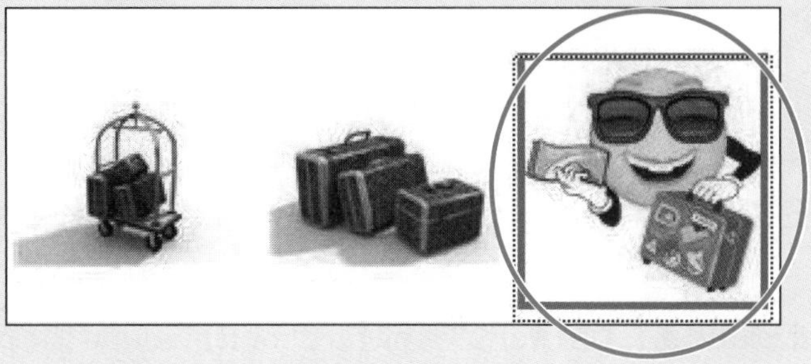

The image should be approximately 2″ wide and 2″ high. If you chose another image, you may need to resize it.

28. Rotate the image to the left approximately **45 degrees**.

Use Newsletter-Style Columns

29. Scroll to **page 1** and position the insertion point in the text below the section break.

30. Lay out the text in two columns with a line between the columns, and then delete the paragraph symbol at the top of the left column.

31. Scroll to **page 3** and position the insertion point in front of the line shown here.

probably·already·has·that·service.·¶

How·does·corporate·demand·look·now?¶

We·feel·really·good·about·what·we're·seeing.·Some·
of·our·best-performing·markets·all·year·were·Boston·

32. Insert a column break, and then turn off formatting marks.

33. Save and close the file; exit **Word**.

34. Submit your final file based on the guidelines provided by your instructor.

To see examples of how your file or files should look at the end of this exercise, go to the student resource center.

Use Building Blocks, Themes, Style Sets, and Drop Caps

Word 2013

In this exercise, you will use one of Word's built-in Building Blocks and create and modify a custom Building Block. You will change the look of your document with a new Theme and Style Set, and you will add a drop cap. Finally, you will use different views and zoom magnifications.

Use Building Blocks

1. Start **Word**. Open **WD08-A02-Merger** from your **WD2013 Lesson 08** folder and save it as **WD08-A02-Merger-[FirstInitialLastName]**.

2. If necessary, choose **Home→Paragraph→Show/Hide** ¶ to display formatting marks.

3. Position the insertion point on the blank line at the top of the left column on page 1.

4. Insert the **Grid Quote** from the **Building Blocks Organizer**, and then type the two lines of text shown in the Grid Quote text box. (The text you type will be capitalized automatically. That's part of the Grid Quote built-in format.)

   ```
   Universal Corporate Events
   January Newsletter
   ```

5. If necessary, position the Building Block so it aligns with the text at the top of the right-hand column.

6. Delete the extra paragraph symbol below the Building Block.
   Now you will create a custom Building Block.

7. Position the insertion point on the blank line at the bottom of the right-hand column on **page 2**.

8. Type the following:

   ```
   Contact us to help you with your corporate travel needs.
   Universal Corporate Events
   123 Highland Avenue
   Chicago, IL 60657
   ```

9. Select the three address lines and remove the after-paragraph spacing.

10. Select the text you typed in **step 8** and save it to the **Quick Part Gallery** as **uce**.

11. Delete the highlighted text in your document, tap [Enter] to create a blank line, and test your Building Block.

12. Modify your Building Block by adding **Suite 2100** at the end of the street address. Use **uce** as the Building Block name again.

13. Delete the Building Block in the document.

14. Test the Building Block. When you're satisfied that it is working as indicated, delete it from the Building Block Organizer so the next student will have the same experience.

15. Leave the updated Building Block at the bottom of the right-hand column on page 2.

Use Themes and Style Sets and Insert a Drop Cap

16. Use **Live Preview** to preview several different Themes and Style Sets.

17. Apply the **Retrospect** Theme to your document.

18. Apply the **Lines (Distinctive)** Style Set.

19. Select the *G* in the first line of the main article and apply a drop cap in the paragraph, not the margin.

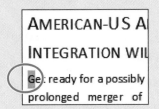

The drop cap is a little too large for the small paragraph, so next you will specify fewer lines for the cap to drop.

20. Make sure the drop cap is selected.

21. Open the **Drop Cap dialog box** using the command shown and change the number of lines to drop to **2**.

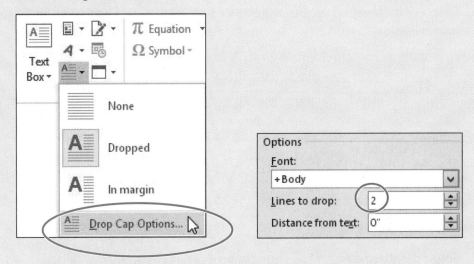

Now that all the formatting is complete, it is a good time to balance the columns on page 2.

22. Position the insertion point at the beginning of the third line of the paragraph shown here (page 2).

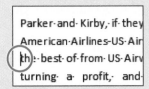

23. Insert a **column break**.

Work with Views and Use Zoom Controls

24. Use the **Read Mode** 📖 button on the status bar to view your document with side-by-side pages.

25. View the entire document by using the arrows on the left and right side of the window.

26. Click the **Web Layout** 🖳 button on the status bar and scroll to see how the document appears.

27. Use the **View** tab to switch back to **Print Layout** 🗏 view.

28. Drag the **Zoom control** on the Zoom bar to set the magnification at **60%**.

29. Click the **Zoom** 🔍 button on the View tab to open the Zoom dialog box. Use the **Many Pages** option to view two pages.

30. Click the **100%** 🔎 button in the Zoom group of the View tab.

31. Turn off formatting marks. Save and close the file; exit **Word**. (If you are prompted to save changes to Building Blocks, click **Don't Save**.)

32. Submit your final file based on the guidelines provided by your instructor.

    To see examples of how your file or files should look at the end of this exercise, go to the student resource center.

APPLY YOUR SKILLS WD08-A03

Create a Columnar Newsletter

In this exercise, you will create a newsletter using columns, graphic elements, Building Blocks, Themes, and Style Sets. Then you will observe your document using various views and zoom magnifications.

Use Section Breaks and WordArt

1. Start **Word**. Open **WD08-A03-TravelTech** from your **WD2013 Lesson 08** folder and save it as WD08-A03-TravelTech-[FirstInitialLastName].

2. If necessary, choose **Home→Paragraph→Show/Hide** ¶ to display formatting marks.

3. Position the insertion point on the third blank line at the top of the document and insert a **continuous section break**.

4. Position the insertion point on the blank line above the section break and type Universal Corporate Events.

5. Select the text, and then open the **WordArt gallery**.

6. Choose **Fill – Black, Text 1, Outline – Background 1, Hard Shadow - Accent 1**.

7. Use the smart tag Layout Options to apply **Top and Bottom wrapping**.

8. With the WordArt selected, apply the **Chevron Up** text effect in the Transform category.

Insert and Format Clip Art

9. Position the insertion point at the end of the first paragraph and tap $\boxed{\text{Enter}}$.

Dear·Corporate·Travel·Agents,¶

Technology·and·mobile·devices·are·more·i
BreakingTravelNews.com·highlights·the·c
Travel·Technology·exhibition·in·Berlin.¶

10. Use **Online Pictures** and **Office.com Clip Art** to search for `mobile device`.

11. Choose the image shown. (If you can't locate this image, choose a similar one.)

12. If necessary, turn on the ruler. Resize the image to approximately **1½ inches wide** and **1½ inches tall**.

13. With the image selected, use **Picture Effects** to apply **Offset Left** in the Shadow category.

14. Crop the image from the left to approximately the point shown.

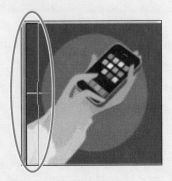

15. Click in the document to turn off the cropping handles.

16. Apply transparent color to the light blue circle in the image. (If you chose a different image, just use the feature for the experience.)

    This did not improve the appearance.

17. Click **Undo**.

Use Newsletter-Style Columns and Building Blocks

18. Apply a **three-column layout** to the body of the newsletter, using lines between columns.

19. Delete the extra paragraph symbol at the top of the first column on the first page.
    Next, you will balance the columns on the second page.

20. Position the insertion point in the second paragraph of the left column (on page 2) and insert a column break, as shown here.

> The·supporting·programme·
> of·the·eTravel·World·(Hall·
> 7.1.c·from·6·to·9·March)·with·
> more·than·50·papers·and·
> workshops·presented·on·two·
> stages·provides·numerous·
> answers·to·these·questions.·
> Topic·headings·at·the·many·
> forums·include·Social·Travel·

21. Position the insertion point in the second paragraph of the right-hand column (on page 2) and insert a column break, as shown here.

> "To·pivot,·or·not·to·pivot,·that·
> is·the·question"·is·the·title·of·
> the·PhoCusWright@ITB·event·

22. Position the insertion point on the second blank line at the bottom of the third column.

23. Insert the **Semaphore Quote** text box from the Building Block Organizer. (You may need to widen the Name column in the organizer to see the full name.)

24. Type the following in the text box. (The text will be capitalized automatically; this is a characteristic of this particular Building Block.)

    Contact Universal Corporate Events at 415-555-1234 to discuss using mobile devices to meet your travel needs.

25. Center the text in the Building Block.

26. Drag the Building Block below the text and center it between the margins.

Use a Theme and a Style Set

27. Open the **Themes** gallery and choose **Retrospect**.

28. Scroll through the document and observe the impact.

29. Open the **Style Set** gallery and choose **Basic (Stylish)** in the Built-In section.

30. Apply a drop cap (Dropped, not In Margin) to the first letter of the main article (page 1, left column).

31. Make any positioning adjustments of graphic images, and insert/ delete any column breaks that you deem necessary.

Use Views and Zoom Controls

32. Turn off formatting marks.

33. Use the **View** tab to observe your document in the following views: **Draft**, **Web Layout**, and **Read Mode**.

34. Use the arrows on the sides of the Read Mode window to scroll through the document.

35. Use the button on the status bar to change to **Print Layout** ☰ view.

36. Click the **Multiple Pages** ⊞ button on the View tab and observe the effect.

37. Use the **Zoom controls** on the status bar to return the document to **100%.**

38. Save and close the file; exit **Word**. (If you are prompted to save changes to Building Blocks, click **Don't Save**.)

39. Submit your final file based on the guidelines provided by your instructor.

Extend Your Skills

In the course of working through the Extend Your Skills exercises, you will think critically as you use the skills taught in the lesson to complete the assigned projects. To evaluate your mastery and completion of the exercises, your instructor may use a rubric, with which more points are allotted according to performance characteristics. (The more you do, the more you earn!) Ask your instructor how your work will be evaluated.

WD08-E01 That's the Way I See It

As a small-business owner, you want to keep your customers interested in what you're doing, so you decide to send out monthly newsletters. Determine the type of business you own and then place a WordArt object with your company's name at the top of a new document. The object should span between the margins (one column). Conduct online research related to your type of business to find information you think will be of interest to your customers. Pull the information into your document, remembering to cite your sources. Lay it out in newsletter-style columns. Insert an image that relates to the content, and use a style from the Picture Styles gallery to enhance the image. Create a custom Building Block that contains contact information for your business, and place it at the end of your newsletter. Place headings within the newsletter, and format them with Word heading styles. Apply a Theme and Style Set of your choice, and insert a drop cap at the beginning of the body text. Be sure to delete your custom Building Block when you are finished so the next student to use the computer will have the same experience. Save your newsletter in your **WD2013 Lesson 08** folder as `WD08-E01-BizLtr-[FirstInitialLastName]`.

You will be evaluated based on the inclusion of all elements specified, your ability to follow directions, your ability to apply newly learned skills to a real-world situation, your creativity, and the relevance of your topic and/or data choice(s). Submit your final file based on the guidelines provided by your instructor.

WD08-E02 Be Your Own Boss

As the owner of Blue Jean Landscaping, you decide to keep in touch with customers by distributing a newsletter. Start a new document, and save it to your **WD2013 Lesson 08** folder as `WD08-E02-Landscape-[FirstInitialLastName]`.

Place the company name at the top of the newsletter using a WordArt style. Insert a continuous section break after the WordArt. Search online for decorative plants and shrubs that can be used for landscaping. Pull in the results of your research as the primary content for the newsletter, ensuring you cite your sources. Format the text in newsletter-style columns.

Insert a picture or clip art image that reflects the newsletter content. Place a three-point border on the images, using a color of your choice. Place a Building Block text box containing contact information at the top of the newsletter. Then, insert headings in the document body formatted with Word heading styles. Apply a Theme and Style Set of your choice. Finally, insert a drop cap at the beginning of the main article.

You will be evaluated based on the inclusion of all elements specified, your ability to follow directions, your ability to apply newly learned skills to a real-world situation, your creativity, and your demonstration of an entrepreneurial spirit. Submit your final file based on the guidelines provided by your instructor.

Transfer Your Skills

In the course of working through the Transfer Your Skills exercises, you will use critical-thinking and creativity skills to complete the assigned projects using skills taught in the lesson. To evaluate your mastery and completion of the exercises, your instructor may use a rubric, with which more points are allotted according to performance characteristics. (The more you do, the more you earn!) Ask your instructor how your work will be evaluated.

WD08-T01 Use the Web as a Learning Tool

Throughout this book, you will be provided with an opportunity to use the Internet as a learning tool by completing WebQuests. According to the original creators of WebQuests, as described on their website (WebQuest.org), a WebQuest is "an inquiry-oriented activity in which most or all of the information used by learners is drawn from the web." To complete the WebQuest projects in this book, navigate to the student resource center for this book and choose the WebQuest for the lesson on which you are currently working. The subject of each WebQuest will be relevant to the material found in the lesson.

WebQuest Subject: Exploring newsletter formatting.

Submit your final file(s) based on the guidelines provided by your instructor.

WD08-T02 Demonstrate Proficiency

Stormy BBQ keeps its customer engaged through a monthly newsletter. This month's newsletter will be about how you cook your barbeque dishes and monthly specials. Conduct online research to gather the primary content for your newsletter, ensuring you cite your sources. Place the name of the business at the top of the newsletter, formatting it with WordArt. Insert a section break to separate the WordArt from the main article. Format the newsletter in columns with a line between. Insert pictures or clip art that enhance your message. Place a text box Building Block at the end of the newsletter that contains the winning recipe from last month's barbeque sauce contest. Insert headings within the newsletter that are formatted with Word heading styles, and apply a Theme and Style Set of your choice. Format the first letter of the main content with a drop cap. Practice viewing your newsletter in various views and zoom magnifications. Save your newsletter in your **WD2013 Lesson 08** folder as `WD08-T02-BBQ-[FirstInitialLastName]`.

Submit your final file based on the guidelines provided by your instructor.

WORD 2013

Creating a Promotional Brochure and a Form

LEARNING OBJECTIVES

After studying this lesson, you will be able to:

- Use shapes to add graphic interest
- Work with SmartArt graphics
- Add page borders and background page color
- Create online forms using form fields

In this lesson, you will add graphic elements to a brochure, such as shapes, which add visual appeal. SmartArt graphics provide a gallery of predesigned diagrams like lists, processes, cycles, hierarchies, and relationships that communicate ideas clearly and vividly. Borders and page color add zing to your brochure. Live preview galleries allow you to quickly test many choices while deciding what looks best for your brochure. You will also create an online registration form that can conveniently be filled out electronically.

Promoting an Ergonomics Seminar

As the owner of Ergonomic Office Solutions, you have decided to create a presentation about the benefits of using ergonomic office equipment. Your friend, Tommy Choi, owner of Green Clean, has provided you with his customer database. Knowing Tommy's customers are already interested in the environment, you believe they would be interested in your products. You decide to create a brochure to mail to local businesses promoting a seminar. You will use product pictures as well as Word's shapes and SmartArt to create a brochure that is both informative and visually appealing. You will also create an online registration form that prospective customers can use to enroll in the seminar. You know that Word's powerful form tools will make it easy to create the form.

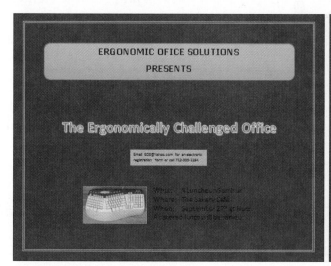
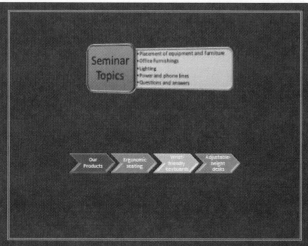

Shapes and pictures add visual interest, and SmartArt graphics engage the reader.

Contact information   2/12/2013
Name   Eugene Washington
Phone   712-555-4321
Email   eugene@yahoo.com

Will you attend the seminar?   Yes ☒ No ☐   What product(s) are you most interested in?
                                                   Ergonomic seating

Would you like to receive our newsletter?   Would you like a free equipment consultation?
Yes ☒ No ☐   Yes ☒ No ☐

Word forms make it easy to enroll in the seminar.

Working with Shapes

Video Library   http://labyrinthelab.com/videos   Video Number: WD13-V0901

Word has a large gallery of graphic shapes, including lines, text boxes, rectangles, ovals, and many others. They can add interest to documents such as flyers and brochures, and you can type text in most shapes. You insert shapes from the Shapes gallery. After you choose a shape, the mouse pointer changes to a crosshair icon resembling a plus sign (+), which you click or drag in the document to create the shape.

FROM THE RIBBON

Insert→Illustrations→
Shapes

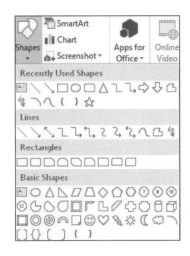

Rotating, Resizing, and Moving Shapes

Clicking a shape displays the handles, which are similar to handles you've seen on other images. You use them to move, resize, or rotate shapes. You can insert a perfect square or circle in one of two ways: by choosing the rectangle or oval tool and clicking in the document, or by holding down Shift while drawing the shape.

The mouse pointer changes shape depending on the action performed or the handle the pointer rests on.

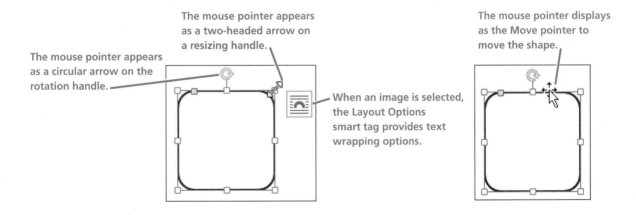

The mouse pointer appears as a two-headed arrow on a resizing handle.

The mouse pointer displays as the Move pointer to move the shape.

The mouse pointer appears as a circular arrow on the rotation handle.

When an image is selected, the Layout Options smart tag provides text wrapping options.

Word 2013

QUICK REFERENCE	WORKING WITH SHAPES
Task	**Procedure**
Insert a perfect square	Choose the rectangle shape, and then click in the document; or, hold Shift while dragging in the document.
Insert a perfect circle	Choose the oval shape, and then click in the document; or, hold Shift while dragging in the document.
Maintain an object's proportions	Hold Shift while dragging a corner resizing handle.
Add text in a shape	Select the shape, and then begin typing.
Select multiple shapes	Hold Shift and click each object.
Align multiple objects	Select objects using Shift, choose Format→Arrange→Align Objects, and choose the desired alignment.
Move an object	Select the object, position the mouse pointer on a border to display the Move pointer, and drag the object as desired.

DEVELOP YOUR SKILLS WD09-D01

Draw, Size, Rotate, and Move Shapes

In this exercise, you will draw different shapes and size, rotate, delete, and move shapes.

1. Open **WD09-D01-Brochure** from your **WD2013 Lesson 09** folder and save it as **WD09-D01-Brochure-[FirstInitialLastName]**.

   Replace the bracketed text with your first initial and last name. For example, if your name is Bethany Smith, your filename would look like this: WD09-D01-Brochure-BSmith.

2. Choose **Design→Document Formatting→Themes** 🅰, and then choose **Office**.

   The change of Theme won't be apparent until you enter more content. Now you will experiment with and insert a shape.

3. Choose **Insert→Illustrations→Shapes** ⬡ to display the Shapes gallery.

4. Choose the **Rounded Rectangle** from the **Rectangles** section.

5. Click and drag anywhere in the document to draw a rounded rectangle.

   The rectangle has a blue fill color, which is related to the Office theme you chose.

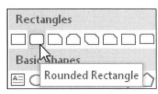

6. Choose **Drawing Tools→Format→Insert Shapes→Shapes** ⬡, and then choose the **Rounded Rectangle** again.

7. Hold the Shift key and drag to draw a rounded rectangle that's larger than the last one.

   Notice that this time you drew a perfect square with rounded corners instead of a rectangle, even though you started with the same shape. This happened because you held down the Shift key while drawing.

Resize and Rotate Shapes

8. With the square shape selected (displaying handles), follow these steps to resize the shape using the handles:

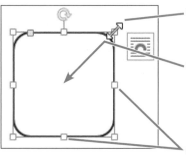

Ⓐ Position the mouse pointer on this sizing handle.

Ⓑ Press ⌷Shift⌷ and drag diagonally toward the center of the shape to resize while maintaining proportions.

Ⓒ Drag from a side handle to change only the length or width of the object.

Ⓓ Click **Undo** so the shape is a square again.

9. Follow these steps to rotate the square:

Ⓐ Position the mouse pointer on the rotation handle; the pointer appears as a circular arrow.

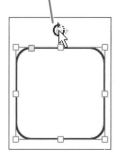
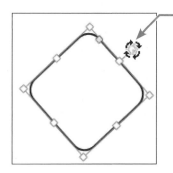

Ⓑ Drag to the right about 45 degrees; the mouse pointer appears as four small arrows when dragging.

10. Experiment with rotation in the opposite direction.

    Next you will delete your practice shapes. You must select a shape before you can delete it.

11. Click one of the shapes to display the handles, and then hold ⌷Shift⌷ and click the other shape.

Holding ⌷Shift⌷ allows you to select multiple shapes at once. Then you can delete, move, or format them all at once.

12. Tap ⌷Delete⌷ to remove both shapes.

Draw a Shape for Your Brochure

13. If necessary, choose **View→Show→Ruler** to display the ruler.

    The Ruler will be helpful in sizing your shape.

14. Choose **Insert→Illustrations→Shapes** ⬦.

15. Choose **Rounded Rectangle** from the Shapes gallery. Starting about 1 inch from the top of the page, draw a wide rectangle at the top margin that spans across the page but remains within the margins. It should be about 1¼ inches high.

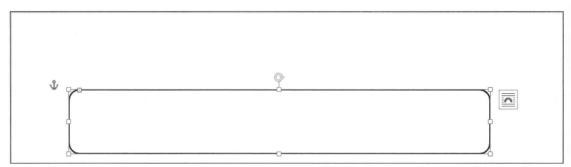

16. Follow these steps to move the shape:

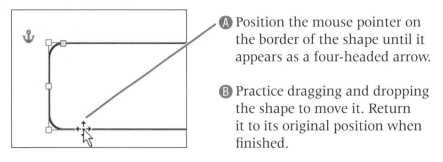

Ⓐ Position the mouse pointer on the border of the shape until it appears as a four-headed arrow.

Ⓑ Practice dragging and dropping the shape to move it. Return it to its original position when finished.

17. Save your file and leave it open.

Adding and Formatting Text in Shapes

Video Library   http://labyrinthelab.com/videos   Video Number: WD13-V0902

You can add text to the shapes you draw. This can be handy if, for example, you want to create a flyer announcing an event. Just select the shape and begin typing. Text is automatically centered, both horizontally and vertically, and it wraps within a shape as you type.

A shape can have either a dotted-line or solid-line border. When the border is a dotted line, you can edit the text. Clicking the dotted-line border changes it to a solid-line border. This means the entire object is selected, and you can change settings that affect everything within the shape.

Formatting Shapes

When a shape is selected, Word provides a contextual Format tab, which contains many tools you can use to add pizzazz to the shape, including shape Styles, Shadow Effects, and 3-D Effects. The Format tab also has its own Insert Shapes gallery containing the same shapes as the Shapes gallery located in the Illustrations group on the Insert tab. When multiple shapes are selected, you can format, resize, or move them simultaneously.

Add Text and Format Text and Shapes

In this exercise, you will add text to a shape and format the text, and then you will format the shape.

1. Save your file as **WD09-D02-Brochure-[FirstInitialLastName]**.

2. If necessary, select the rectangle shape at the top margin.

3. Tap ⌈Caps Lock⌉, type **ERGONOMIC OFFICE SOLUTIONS**, tap ⌈Enter⌉, and type **PRESENTS**. *Notice that the text was automatically centered in the shape.*

4. Click the border of the shape, taking care not to drag.

Selecting a shape by the border selects everything inside the shape. Thus, the text in the shape is selected, although it is not highlighted.

5. Choose **Home→Font→Font menu ▼,** and then choose **Tahoma**.

6. Keep the shape selected and apply **Bold 22 pt** font.

7. If your shape is not big enough for the larger text, drag a sizing handle to enlarge it. *Next, you will use the Shape Styles gallery to format the shape.*

8. Make sure the object is selected so the contextual Format tab is available.

9. Choose **Drawing Tools→Format→Shape Styles**.

10. Follow these steps to format the shape:

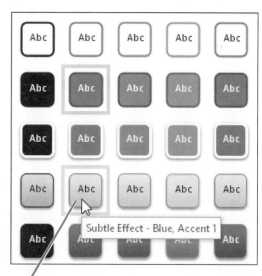

Ⓐ Click the **More** button to open the Shape Styles gallery.

Ⓑ Choose **Subtle Effect – Blue, Accent 1**.

11. Save your file.

Aligning Objects

Video Library http://labyrinthelab.com/videos Video Number: WD13-V0903

You can drag and drop objects to align them, but using the Align Objects feature on the contextual Format tab is more precise. You select the objects you want to align and then choose the desired alignment.

DEVELOP YOUR SKILLS WD09-D03
Align Objects

In this exercise, you will add a WordArt object and align it with a shape. You will insert a picture into a preexisting table, and format and move the table.

1. Save your file as **WD09-D03-Brochure-[FirstInitialLastName]**.

2. Click in the document below the rectangle.

3. Choose **Insert→Text→Insert WordArt** [A].

4. Choose **Fill – Blue, Accent 1, Outline – Background 1, Hard Shadow – Accent1**, and then type **The Ergonomically Challenged Office**.

5. Place the mouse pointer on the border of the WordArt object, and then drag to position it about 1 inch below the rectangle.
   Don't worry about centering it below the shape; you will align the objects in the next steps.

Align Objects

6. With the WordArt object still selected, hold down ⌷Shift⌷ and click **Round Rectangle**.
   Both objects should be selected—handles appear on both.

7. Choose **Drawing Tools→Format→Arrange→Align Objects** [▣], and then choose **Align Center**.
   This center-aligns the objects with each other.

8. If necessary, drag the selected objects so they are centered between the margins.

9. Click in the document to deselect the objects.

Insert a Picture in the Brochure

10. Scroll down, and position the insertion point in the left cell of the table.

11. Choose **Insert→Illustrations→Pictures** .

12. Navigate to the **WD2013 Lesson 09** folder and double-click the **WD09-D03-Keyboard** file to insert it.

13. Using the left margin area, click to select the table row.

14. Position the mouse pointer on the line between the two cells and double-click to resize both columns to their best fit.

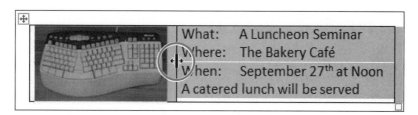

15. Position the mouse pointer on the table's **move handle** , and then drag to the right to center the table under the other objects.

16. If necessary, select the table again. Then, choose **Home→Paragraph→Borders** menu ▼.

17. Choose **No Border** to complete the page.

ERGONOMIC OFFICE SOLUTIONS

PRESENTS

The Ergonomically Challenged Office

What:	A Luncheon Seminar
Where:	The Bakery Café
When:	September 27th at Noon
A catered lunch will be served	

18. If gridlines appear in the table (although they won't print), follow these steps to remove them. Otherwise, go to the next step.

   ■ Make sure the table is selected.

   ■ Choose **Table Tools→Layout→Table→View Gridlines** [icon].

19. Save your file.

Working with Text Boxes

A text box is a special type of shape designed for you to insert text or graphics. You may wonder how inserting a text box is different from drawing a shape and adding text inside it. It's because of the formatting. For example, when you apply a theme to a document, the theme includes formatting such as fill and line colors for shapes. Text boxes do not contain those formatting characteristics; you type in it, there is no fill color, and the text entered is left-aligned, starting at the top of the box. You can format all of the text by selecting the text box itself, or format only a portion of the text by selecting the part you want to change.

Adding a Text Box

A text box tool appears in the Shapes gallery as shown in the following illustration.

As with other shapes, you either click to place a text box in the document or drag it to the desired size. You can also use the Text Box gallery in the Text group (Insert tab) to draw a text box or choose a preformatted one from the gallery. If you insert the text box by clicking in the document, the text box widens to the edge of the paper as you type and then begins to wrap the text. However, if you drag to draw the text box, it remains the same size. But you can resize with a sizing handle if needed.

Formatting a Text Box

You can format a text box just like any other object. You must select the text box before you can change the line surrounding it, change the fill color, resize it, or perform any other options available on the contextual Format tab.

QUICK REFERENCE	WORKING WITH TEXT BOXES
Task	**Procedure**
Insert a text box	Choose Insert→Illustrations→Shapes→Text Box, and then click in the document or drag to draw to the desired size; or, choose Insert→Text→Text Box and choose a preformatted text box or choose Draw Text Box.
Format a text box	Select the text box and choose the desired formatting commands from the Format tab.

Work with Text Boxes

In this exercise, you will insert a text box, reposition it, and format the text within it.

1. Save your file as **WD09-D04-Brochure-[FirstInitialLastName]**.

2. Choose **Insert→Illustrations→Shapes** ⬦, and then choose **Text Box** ▣ from the Shapes gallery.

3. Position the mouse pointer below the WordArt object, and then drag to draw a text box about **2¾ inches wide** and **½ inch tall**.

4. Type the text shown here. If necessary, size the text box so the text wrapping is the same as that shown.

> Email EOS@Yahoo.com for an electronic
> registration form or call 712-555-1234.

5. If the email address appears as a hyperlink, click in the hyperlink, and then right-click it and choose **Remove Hyperlink**.

   Now you'll format the text box.

6. Make sure the text box is selected.

7. Choose **Drawing Tools→Format→Shape Styles→Shape Outline** ✎ and choose **No Outline**.

8. Choose **Drawing Tools→Format→Shape Styles→Shape Fill** ⬧ and choose **Blue, Accent 1, Lighter 40%**.

9. With the text box still selected, hold down ⎇Shift and select the two objects above it.

10. Choose **Drawing Tools→Format→Arrange→Align Objects** ⬛ and choose **Align Center**.

11. Click in the document to deselect the three objects.

12. Save your file.

Working with SmartArt

Video Library   http://labyrinthelab.com/videos   Video Number: WD13-V0905

It's often easier to grasp concepts if information is presented graphically rather than textually. Word provides a large variety of SmartArt graphics that you can add to documents. They make it easy to combine predesigned graphics with text to create sophisticated figures. The SmartArt Graphic dialog box contains a large array of graphic images.

Choosing a category displays the associated images in the center pane.

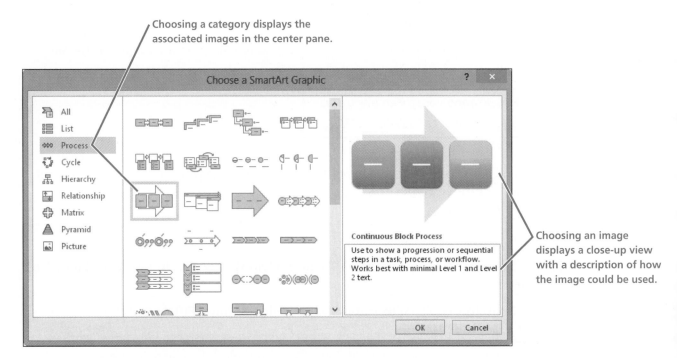

Choosing an image displays a close-up view with a description of how the image could be used.

SmartArt Categories

SmartArt images are divided into the following categories:

Category	Purpose
List	Shows nonsequential data
Process	Shows steps in a process or progression
Cycle	Shows a continual process
Hierarchy	Creates a hierarchical structure or shows a decision tree
Relationship	Illustrates associations
Matrix	Shows how parts relate to a whole
Pyramid	Shows proportional relationships
Picture	Used when you want to convey your message with or without explanatory text, or when you want to use pictures to complement a list or process

Using the SmartArt Text Pane

You use a SmartArt text pane to add text to your image. When you insert the image, the text pane may or may not be open. If the pane is not open, click the tab that appears on the left side of the image. The same tab closes the text pane. The [Text] placeholders are replaced with the text you enter in the SmartArt text pane.

SmartArt text pane ⎯⎯⎯⎯⎯⎯⎯⎯⎯⎯⎯⎯ Tab that opens or closes the text pane

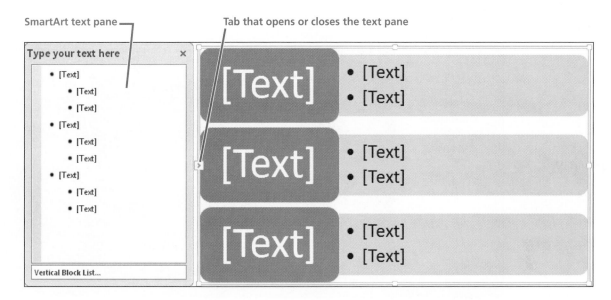

You type in a bulleted list in the Type Your Text Here pane as shown in the preceding illustration. As you type, the text is added to the image. Word adjusts the font size based on the amount of information you type.

You can also type directly in the graphic, just like typing in a shape.

Modifying SmartArt

If you cannot find the exact image you want, you can modify, add, and delete shapes within the graphic. SmartArt objects are formatted in the same way as other graphic shapes.

As you enter and format text here, it appears in the graphic.

You can select objects within a graphic if you wish to format or resize them separately.

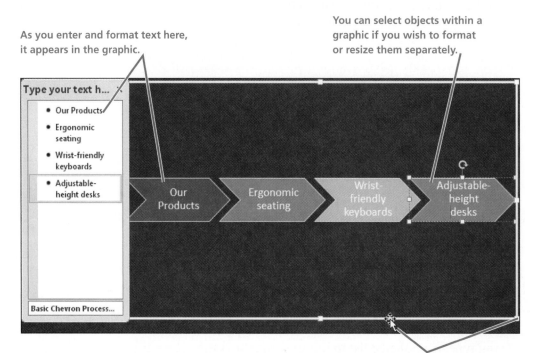

You can position the mouse pointer on the border to display the move handle, or you can drag a handle to resize.

QUICK REFERENCE	USING SMARTART
Task	**Procedure**
Insert a SmartArt image	Choose Insert→Illustrations→SmartArt, select the desired category, choose the desired object, and click OK.
Add text to a SmartArt object	If necessary, click the tab on the left side of the image, use the text pane to add text to the object, or type directly in the shape.
Apply a SmartArt Style	Choose SmartArt Tools→Design→SmartArt Styles and choose the desired style.

Insert SmartArt

In this exercise, you will use two SmartArt graphics: one to list the seminar topics and one to list the ergonomic products. You will customize and resize the graphics.

1. Save your file as **WD09-D05-Brochure-[FirstInitialLastName]**.

2. Press Ctrl + End to move the insertion point to the bottom of the document.

3. Press Ctrl + Enter to insert a page break.

4. Choose **Home→Paragraph→Center** 📄.
   Your image will be center-aligned when you insert it.

Insert SmartArt

5. Choose **Insert→Illustrations→SmartArt** 📇.

6. Follow these steps to insert a SmartArt object:

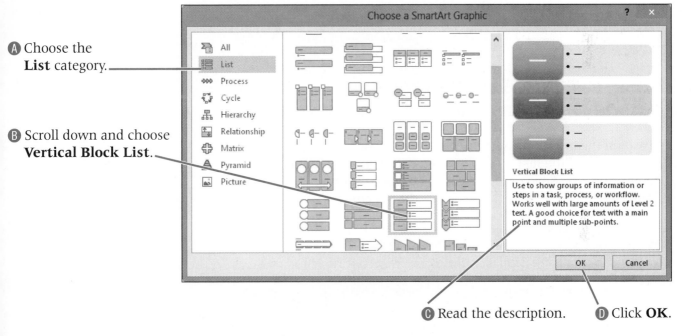

Ⓐ Choose the **List** category.

Ⓑ Scroll down and choose **Vertical Block List**.

Ⓒ Read the description.

Ⓓ Click **OK**.

7. If the text pane is not visible, click the tab.

Word 2013

Customize the Image

This image has three major text objects, but you will only use one.

8. Position the mouse pointer to the left of the first major bullet, and then drag down to select the first six bullets.

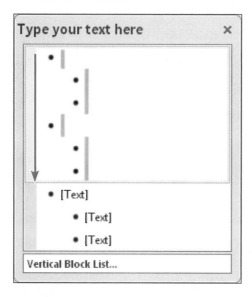

9. Tap ⌈Delete⌉ to remove the bullets.

10. Follow these steps to begin entering the seminar topics:

Ⓐ Position the insertion point to the right of the first bullet and type **Seminar Topics**.

Ⓑ Tap ⌈↓⌉ on the keyboard and type **Placement of equipment and furniture**.

Ⓒ Notice that the text appears in the graphic as you type.

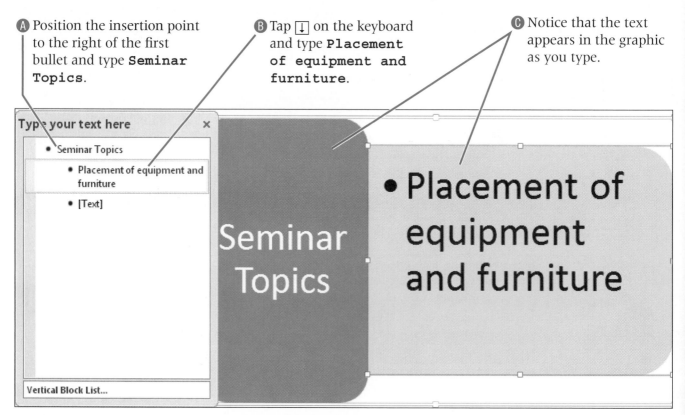

11. Tap ↓ to go to the next line, and type **Office furnishings**.

12. Tap Enter to generate the next bullet, and then type **Lighting**.

13. Tap Enter as necessary, and then type the following items to complete the list:
    - **Power and phone lines**
    - **Questions and answers**

14. Click the **Close** ✕ button in the upper-right corner of the Type Your Text Here pane.

15. Click the outside border frame to make sure the *entire* SmartArt image is selected.
    You will resize the SmartArt object next. If an object within the main frame is selected, you could accidentally resize only a part of the SmartArt object. Clicking the outside border frame prevents that.

16. Drag the bottom-center sizing handle up until the image is approximately half as tall as the original image.

17. Save your file.

Changing a SmartArt Style

Video Library   http://labyrinthelab.com/videos   Video Number: WD13-V0906

The SmartArt Styles gallery provides interesting variations of the original graphic. Live Preview lets you see the effect of the various styles without actually applying them.

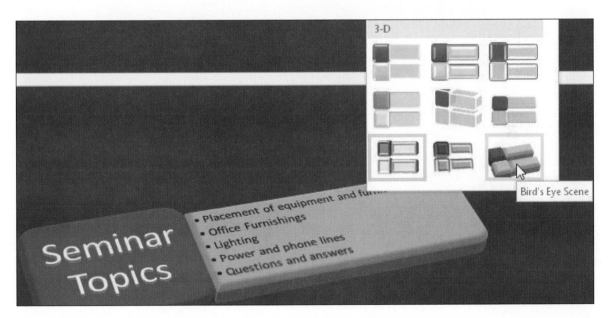

Apply a SmartArt Style

In this exercise, you will customize SmartArt graphics by applying colors and styles.

1. Save your file as **WD09-D06-Brochure-[FirstInitialLastName]**.

2. Make sure the SmartArt image is selected.

3. Choose **SmartArt Tools→Design→SmartArt Styles→Change Colors** .

4. In the Accent 1 category, choose **Gradient Loop – Accent 1**.

5. Choose **SmartArt Tools→Design→SmartArt Styles→More ⏷ button** to display the entire gallery.

6. In the 3-D category, choose **Metallic Scene**.
   Next you will add another SmartArt image.

7. Press Ctrl + End to move to the end of the document, and then tap Enter twice.

8. Choose **Insert→Illustrations→SmartArt** .

9. Follow these steps to insert the next image:

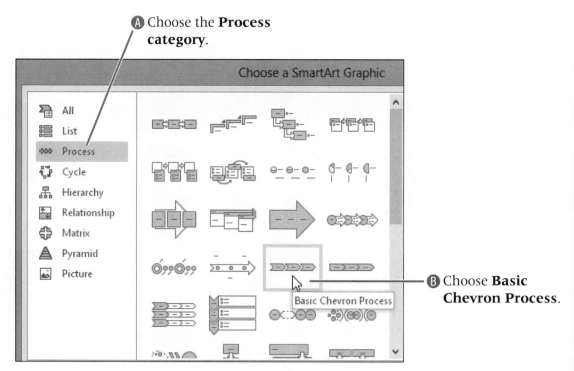

Ⓐ Choose the **Process category**.

Ⓑ Choose **Basic Chevron Process**.

10. Click **OK** to insert the image.

Type in the Graphic Image

11. Click the **[Text] placeholder** in the first arrow and type `Our products`.

You can type directly in the image without opening the text pane.

12. Click in each arrow and enter the text shown in the following illustration.

13. With the image selected, follow these steps to add an arrow:

Ⓐ Click the tab to open the text pane.

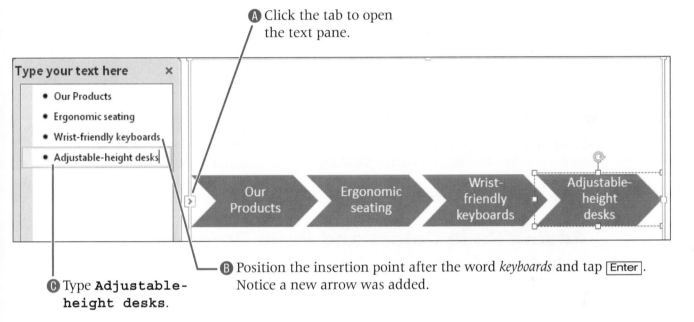

Ⓑ Position the insertion point after the word *keyboards* and tap Enter. Notice a new arrow was added.

Ⓒ Type **Adjustable-height desks**.

14. **Close** × the text pane.

Format the Image

15. With the shape selected, choose **SmartArt Tools→Design→SmartArt Styles→Change Colors**.

16. Choose the fourth item in the Accent 1 category, **Gradient Loop – Accent 1**.

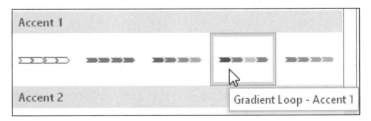

17. Click the **More** button on the SmartArt Styles gallery. In the 3-D category, choose **Cartoon**.

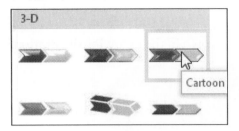

18. Click in the document to deselect the image.

19. Save the file.

Formatting the Page Background

Video Library   http://labyrinthelab.com/videos   Video Number: WD13-V0907

Word has great page background formats that add color and visual variety to your documents. Page colors and borders provide the finishing touches that add professional polish and pizzazz. For example, you can add colors from a gallery specifically designed to blend with a document's theme. Border theme colors are also designed to tastefully complement page colors.

Adding Page Colors and Page Borders

The Page Colors gallery is similar to other galleries you have worked with. The colors that appear in the Theme Colors section of the gallery, as the name implies, are based on the Theme currently in effect.

Page borders surround the outer edges of the entire page. You can adjust the color (again, based on the current Theme), line thickness, and other features of the border.

The Borders and Shading Dialog Box

This dialog box allows you to make settings similar to those you can set for paragraph borders.

A variety of border line styles appear here.

This area lets you specify which sides of a border you wish to apply to the page.

You can choose a predesigned border style, or you can opt to create a custom border.

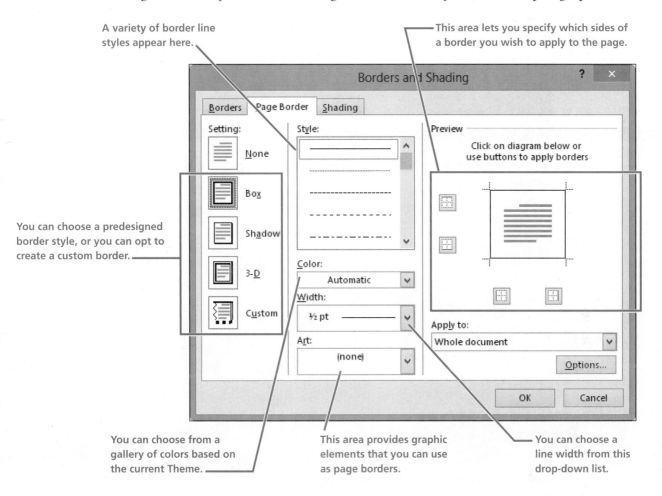

You can choose from a gallery of colors based on the current Theme.

This area provides graphic elements that you can use as page borders.

You can choose a line width from this drop-down list.

Inserting a Watermark

A watermark is text or a graphic that is placed behind the text or other objects in a document; it is visible only in Page Layout or Read Mode view. Some common watermarks include a faint image of the word *Draft* or *Confidential* in the background.

This is an example of a watermark. Notice the word *Draft* in the background.

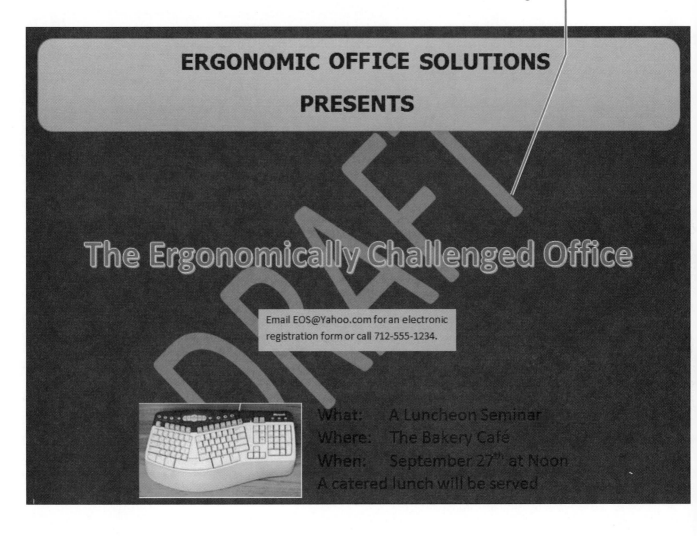

There are built-in text watermarks, or you can create your own custom text. A clip art image or picture can also be used as a watermark.

You can choose this option to insert a picture as a watermark.

You can customize a watermark with your own text.

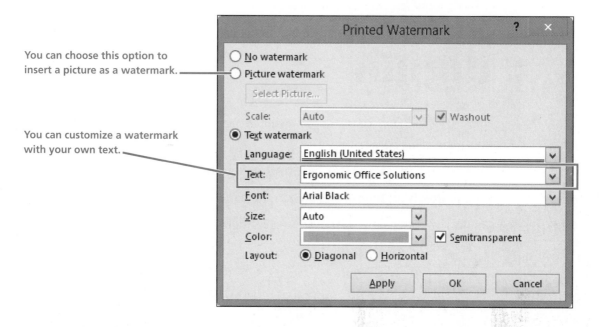

QUICK REFERENCE	FORMATTING PAGE BACKGROUNDS
Task	**Procedure**
Add a page color	■ Choose Design→Page Background→Page Color and choose the desired color.
Add a page border	■ Choose Design→Page Background→Page Borders and choose the desired style, color, width, and other options.
Add a watermark	■ Choose Design→Page Background→Watermark and choose the desired watermark or Custom Watermark.

Apply a Page Color, Page Border, and Watermark

In this exercise, you will add a background color to your brochure and a border surrounding the pages. Finally, you will add a Draft watermark to the document.

1. Save your file as **WD09-D07-Brochure-[FirstInitialLastName]**.

2. Choose **Design→Page Background→Page Color** .

3. Hover the mouse pointer over several colors in the Theme Colors area of the gallery, and Live Preview displays the effects of the different colors.

4. Choose the color in the fifth column, bottom row, **Blue**, **Accent 1**, **Darker 50%**.

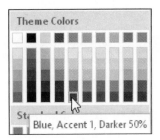

Now you'll add a page border.

5. Choose **Design→Page Background→Page Borders** .

6. Choose **Box** from the Setting area in the panel on the left.

7. Follow these steps to format the page border:

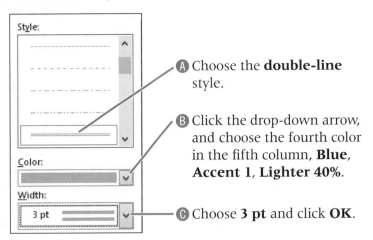

ⓐ Choose the **double-line** style.

ⓑ Click the drop-down arrow, and choose the fourth color in the fifth column, **Blue**, **Accent 1**, **Lighter 40%**.

ⓒ Choose **3 pt** and click **OK**.

Now you will add a Draft watermark, and then finalize the document by removing it.

8. Choose **Design→Page Background→Watermark**, and then choose **Draft 1** from the gallery.

9. Scroll through the document to view the watermark, page border, and page color on both pages.

10. **Undo** to remove the watermark from the document.

11. Save and close your file.

Working with Forms

Word 2013

Video Library   http://labyrinthelab.com/videos   Video Number: WD13-V0908

Many organizations use forms to collect data. Forms contain both fields, where users enter information, and objects, such as checkboxes and drop-down lists, to assist users with data entry. With Word, you can easily set up forms to meet the needs of your organization and distribute them in any of the following formats:

- **Printed:** Printed forms are produced and filled out on paper.
- **Electronic:** Non-printed forms are distributed to Word users and filled out in Word. They are often available via a network or sent in an email.
- **Internet-Based:** These forms are posted to a website and filled out using a web browser. The data is stored in an electronic database. Word lets you set up forms and save them as web pages.

Setting Up Forms

You can set up forms using the same tools and techniques used to create any other type of document. However, tables are often used because they allow you to lay out forms with an orderly structure. Creating a form in a table is much easier than using tabs. Word also provides special form fields.

DEVELOP YOUR SKILLS WD09-D08
Set Up the Form

In this exercise, you will use a table as the basis for the form, and you'll add custom tab stops to align form fields. You will use the form to enroll prospective customers in The Ergonomically Challenged Office seminar.

1. Open **WD09-D08-Registration** from the **WD2013 Lesson 09** folder and save it as `WD09-D08-Registration-[FirstInitialLastName]`.

2. If necessary, click the **Show/Hide** ¶ button to turn on formatting marks.
   The formatting marks make it easier for you to see exactly what you are doing in the form.

3. If necessary, choose **View→Show→Ruler** to display the ruler.

4. Check that Left Tab is active in the Tabs box. If not, click the **Tabs box** at the left end of the ruler until it displays a symbol that resembles an uppercase L.
   You will be setting left tabs in the form.

5. Click in the first table cell, and then follow these steps to begin adding text to the form:

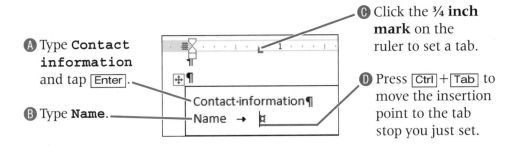

A Type **Contact information** and tap Enter.

B Type **Name**.

C Click the ¾ **inch mark** on the ruler to set a tab.

D Press Ctrl + Tab to move the insertion point to the tab stop you just set.

You will insert a form field at this position in the next exercise.

Press Ctrl + Tab to move the insertion point *within* a cell; tap Tab to move the insertion point to the *next* cell.

6. Save your file.

Understanding Form Fields

Video Library   http://labyrinthelab.com/videos   Video Number: WD13-V0909

Fields in a form are made up of controls. There are three types of controls you can use in a form: content controls, legacy forms, and ActiveX controls. The type of document you are creating, and who will be using it, determine which control set to use in the form. See the following table for descriptions of each type of control.

FORM CONTROLS	
Type	**Description**
Content Controls	These controls were introduced in Word 2007. The group contains controls that did not exist in the legacy tools. These controls have limitations on data-restriction properties. For example, you can insert a Plain Text Content Control, but there is no option to limit the maximum length for the entry.
Legacy Forms	This older set of form fields is still available. This set does not include the newer controls, such as the Date Picker and Picture controls, but these fields can be used in any Word version and allow data restrictions to be set.
ActiveX Controls	This set of controls is reserved for documents used in a web page.

The Developer Tab

All three types of controls are found in the Developer tab, which does not appear on the Ribbon by default. You must activate it by placing a checkmark next to Developer in the Word Options dialog box, as shown in the following illustration. The three types of controls in the Developer tab appear on the right.

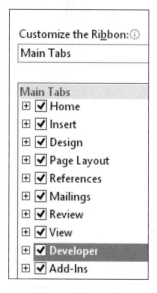

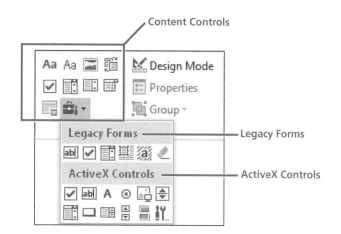

Content Controls

Legacy Forms

ActiveX Controls

QUICK REFERENCE	INSERTING FORM FIELDS
Task	**Procedure**
Insert a content control in a form	Choose Developer→Controls and choose the desired content control.
Insert a form field from the Legacy Tools	Choose Developer→Controls→Legacy Tools and choose the desired form field.

Using the Form

After you create the form, you must protect it in order to activate the form fields so users can enter data. You will protect the form later in the lesson.

DEVELOP YOUR SKILLS WD09-D09
Insert Form Fields

In this exercise, you will display the Developer tab. You will then use a combination of content controls and legacy forms controls to insert text fields, a date field, checkboxes, and drop-down fields in your document.

1. Save your file as **WD09-D09-Registration-[FirstInitialLastName]**.

2. Right-click the **Home** tab and choose **Customize the Ribbon**.

3. Place a checkmark in the **Developer** checkbox.

4. Click **OK** to display the Developer tab.

5. If necessary, click **Show/Hide** ¶ to turn on the formatting marks.

6. If necessary, position the insertion point at the ¾ **inch tab stop** in the second line of the first cell.

Insert Form Fields

All form fields in this form will come from the Legacy Forms controls, except the date field.

7. Choose **Developer→Controls**.

8. Follow these steps to insert a legacy Text Form Field:

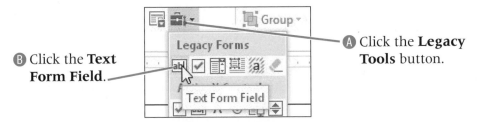

Ⓑ Click the **Text Form Field**.

Ⓐ Click the **Legacy Tools** button.

If formatting marks and shading are turned on, the form field displays small circles and shading.

9. If a shaded box is not visible, follow these steps; otherwise, go to the next step.
   - Choose **Developer→Controls→Legacy Tools** 🧰.
   - Choose **Form Field Shading** 🇦.

10. Tap ⎣Enter⎦ and type **Phone**.

11. Press ⎣Ctrl⎦+⎣Tab⎦ and insert another **Text Form Field**.

12. Tap ⎣Enter⎦ and type **Email**.

13. Press ⎣Ctrl⎦+⎣Tab⎦ and insert another **Text Form Field**.

Insert a Content Control

14. Tap `Tab` to move to the next table cell.

15. Choose **Home→Paragraph→Align Right** ☰.

16. Choose **Developer→Controls→Date Picker Content Control** ⊞. (This is not a legacy tool.)

Your form should now look like the following illustration.

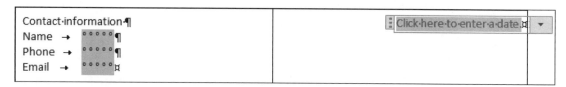

17. Save your file.

Using the Checkbox and Drop-Down List

Video Library http://labyrinthelab.com/videos   Video Number: WD13-V0910

In addition to a Text Form Field, Word provides a Check Box Form Field and a Drop-Down Form Field. Drop-down fields allow you to enter specific choices to be displayed in a list, while checkboxes restrict answers to a yes/no type of response.

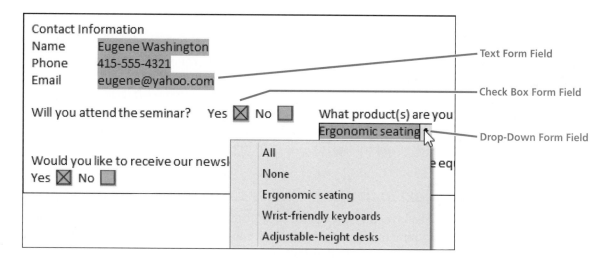

DEVELOP YOUR SKILLS WD09-D10

Add Checkboxes and Drop-Down Lists

In this exercise, you will continue adding form fields to the document, including checkboxes and drop-down lists.

1. Save your file as **WD09-D10-Registration-[FirstInitialLastName]**.

2. Position the insertion point in the first cell of the second row.

3. Type **Will you attend the seminar?**

4. Click the **2-inch mark** on the ruler to set a left tab and press [Ctrl] + [Tab].

5. Type **Yes** and tap [Spacebar] twice.

6. Choose **Developer→Controls→Legacy Tools** 🛠 and choose **Check Box Form Field** ☑.

7. Tap [Spacebar] twice, type **No**, and then tap [Spacebar] twice.

8. Insert another **Legacy Check Box Form Field** ☑.

9. Tap [Tab] to move to the next table cell.

10. Type **What product(s) are you most interested in?** and tap [Enter].

11. Choose **Developer→Controls→Legacy Tools** then **Drop-Down Form Field** 📋.

12. Tap [Tab] to move to the next table cell.

13. Insert Legacy text and checkboxes in the last row as shown, tapping [Enter] and [Spacebar] as indicated.

Would·you·like·to·receive·our·newsletter?¶ Yes·■··No··■¤	Would·you·like·a·free·equipment·consultation?¶ Yes··■··No··■¤

14. Save your file.

Applying Field Properties

Video Library   http://labyrinthelab.com/videos   Video Number: WD13-V0911

Each field type has various form field properties associated with it. For example, you can restrict the type and set the maximum length for data entered in text fields. You can have Word automatically format a date to a particular format. Although you cannot prevent all errors during data entry, property restrictions help in that effort.

Modifying Text in the Date Picker Content Control and Legacy Fields

Default text is displayed in the Date Picker Content Control when you insert it. You can modify the default text by typing over it. When the form is used, the text in the control is replaced when the user selects the date from the calendar icon that appears when the user clicks the field's drop-down arrow.

Legacy fields use the form field options dialog boxes to modify properties. Options in the dialog boxes vary based on the field selected.

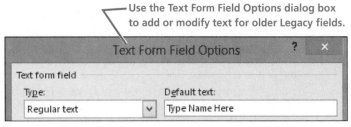
Use the Text Form Field Options dialog box to add or modify text for older Legacy fields.

Type over default text in the Date Picker Content Control to replace it.

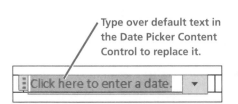

QUICK REFERENCE	APPLYING FIELD PROPERTIES
Task	**Procedure**
Modify text in the Date Picker Content Control	▪ Type over the text in the control.
Set field properties for legacy form fields	▪ Select the field and choose Developer→Controls→Properties, or double-click the form field. ▪ Make the desired choices in the Form Field Options dialog box.

DEVELOP YOUR SKILLS WD09-D11
Set Field Properties

In this exercise, you will set field properties for the various field types and finish formatting the table.

1. Save your file as **WD09-D11-Registration-[FirstInitialLastName]**.

2. Follow these steps to add default instruction text to the Name field:

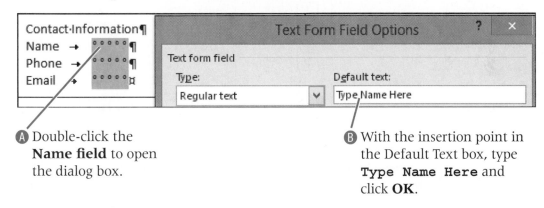

Ⓐ Double-click the **Name field** to open the dialog box.

Ⓑ With the insertion point in the Default Text box, type **Type Name Here** and click **OK**.

3. Use the same process to add text to the **Phone** and **Email** fields.
   - ▪ Phone: **Type Phone Number Here**
   - ▪ Email: **Type Email Address Here**

4. Select the default text in the date field at the top of the right-hand column and type **Click arrow; select today's date**.

Set List Properties

5. Double-click the field in the right-hand column of the second row.

6. Type **All** in the **Drop-Down Item box** and click **Add**.

7. Type **None** in the **Drop-Down Item box** and click **Add**.

8. Use the same process to add the remaining items to the list.

   - `Ergonomic seating`
   - `Wrist-friendly keyboards`
   - `Adjustable-height desks`

9. Click **OK**.

Finalize the Appearance of the Form

10. Select the table, choose **Home→Paragraph→Borders ⊞ menu ▼**, and choose **Borders and Shading**.

11. Follow these steps to format the borders:

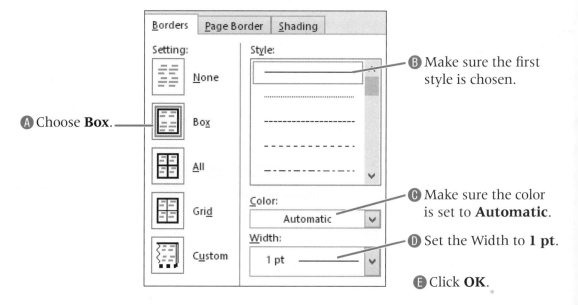

12. If necessary, with the table selected, choose **Table Tools→Layout→Table→View Gridlines** to turn off gridlines.

13. If necessary, choose **Home→Paragraph→Show/Hide ¶** to turn off formatting marks.

14. Choose **Developer→Controls→Legacy Tools→Form Field Shading ⓐ** to turn off shading.

15. Save your file.

Protecting Forms

Video Library http://labyrinthelab.com/videos Video Number: WD13-V0912

The Restrict Editing feature can prevent users from making changes other than in the form fields. Protecting forms also triggers the form fields to behave like form fields. For example, clicking a checkbox will insert or remove an X. You unprotect a form when designing or modifying it, and you protect it when you are ready to use it.

QUICK REFERENCE	PROTECTING FORMS
Task	**Procedure**
Protect a form	■ Choose Developer→Protect→Restrict Editing.
	■ In the Restrict Editing task pane, check the Allow Only This Type of Editing in the Document checkbox.
	■ Choose Filling in Forms from the drop-down list and click Yes, Start Enforcing Protection.
	■ Add and confirm a password, and click OK. Or, leave the password fields blank and click OK.
Stop protection	■ Click the Stop Protection button in the Restrict Editing task pane, enter a password if prompted, and click OK.

Distributing and Using Forms

You can simply print and distribute paper forms to users. Electronic forms are typically distributed via email. Users can complete an electronic form in Word and return the completed form to the person responsible for collecting the data.

DEVELOP YOUR SKILLS WD09-D12
Protect and Use the Form

In this exercise, you will protect the form and enter data in the special form fields. You will also finalize the table formatting and turn off the Developer tab.

1. Save your file as **WD09-D12-Registration-[FirstInitialLastName]**.

2. Choose **Developer→Protect→Restrict Editing** 🔒.

   The Restrict Editing task pane opens.

3. Follow these steps to protect the form:

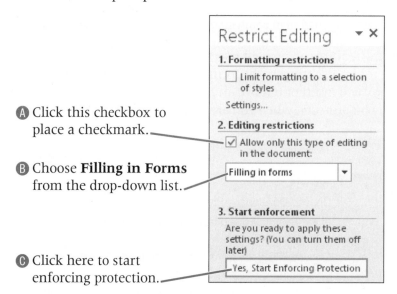

Ⓐ Click this checkbox to place a checkmark.

Ⓑ Choose **Filling in Forms** from the drop-down list.

Ⓒ Click here to start enforcing protection.

4. You won't set a password, so click **OK** to dismiss the password dialog box.

5. Tap Tab twice to move the insertion point from field to field.

You cannot tab out of a content-control field, such as the Date Picker Content Control; you must click or use the arrow keys.

6. Press Shift + Tab twice to move backwards to the **Name** field.

Fill Out the Form

7. Type **Eugene Washington** and tap Tab.

8. Type **712-555-4321** and tap Tab.

9. Type **eugene@yahoo.com** and tap Tab.

10. Follow these steps to insert the date:

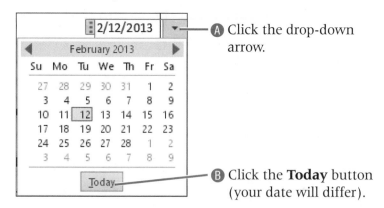

Ⓐ Click the drop-down arrow.

Ⓑ Click the **Today** button (your date will differ).

11. In the second table row, click **Yes**.

12. Follow these steps to make a choice from the drop-down field.

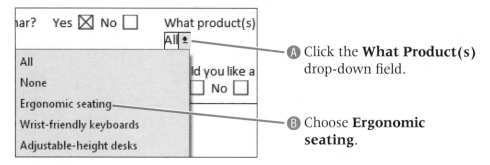

Ⓐ Click the **What Product(s)** drop-down field.

Ⓑ Choose **Ergonomic seating**.

13. In the last row, click both **Yes** checkboxes.

Your form should now look like the following illustration. The date will vary.

Contact information Name Eugene Washington Phone 712-555-4321 Email eugene@yahoo.com	2/12/2013
Will you attend the seminar? Yes ☒ No ☐	What product(s) are you most interested in? Ergonomic seating
Would you like to receive our newsletter? Yes ☒ No ☐	Would you like a free equipment consultation? Yes ☒ No ☐

Stop Protection

14. Click the **Stop Protection** button in the Restrict Editing task pane, and then close it.

15. Right-click the **Home** tab and choose **Customize the Ribbon**.

16. Remove the checkmark from the **Developer** checkbox and click **OK**.

17. Save and close your file. Exit **Word**.

Concepts Review

To check your knowledge of the key concepts introduced in this lesson, complete the Concepts Review quiz by choosing the appropriate access option below.

If you are...	Then access the quiz by...
Using the Labyrinth Video Library	Going to http://labyrinthelab.com/videos
Using eLab	Logging in, choosing Content, and navigating to the Concepts Review quiz for this lesson
Not using the Labyrinth Video Library or eLab	Going to the student resource center for this book

Reinforce Your Skills

Use Shapes, SmartArt, and Add Page Color and a Border

In this exercise, you will create a certificate using graphic Shapes and SmartArt, and then you will format the certificate background with a page color and a page border.

Work with Shapes

1. Start **Word**. Create a new document based on the **Blank Document template** and save it in your **WD2013 Lesson 09** folder as `WD09-R01-Certificate-[FirstInitialLastName]`.

2. Choose **Page Layout→Page Setup→Orientation**, and then choose **Landscape**.

3. If necessary, choose **Home→Paragraph→Show/Hide ¶** to display formatting marks.

4. Tap Enter fifteen times.
   It can be easier to work with graphics if some spacing is already set up.

5. Choose **Design→Document Formatting→Themes**, and then choose the **Slice** Theme.

6. If necessary, choose **View→Views→Ruler** to turn on the ruler.

7. Choose **Insert→Illustrations→Shapes**. In the Stars and Banners category, choose **Down Ribbon**.

8. Position the mouse pointer, which appears as a crosshair, next to the paragraph symbol at the top of the page.

9. Press and hold the mouse button, drag to the right until the image is about **6 inches wide**, and drag down until the image is approximately **2 inches high**.

10. Type `Outstanding Member` in the image.

11. Click the border of the image to select the entire image.

12. Choose **Home→Font**, choose **Comic Sans MS**, **28 pt**, and click **Bold B**.

13. Choose **Home→Font→Font Color ▼ menu button**, and choose **Red** in the Standard Colors section.

14. If necessary, drag the object to center it between the margins.

15. Click in the document to deselect the image.

Work with Text Boxes

16. Choose **Insert→Illustration→Shapes** , and then choose **Text Box** from the Basic Shapes category.

17. Position the mouse pointer approximately one inch below the other graphic, and draw a text box that is approximately **5 inches wide and 1 inch tall**.

18. Enter the following text in the text box:

    ```
    Janisha Robinson
    Second Quarter: Most Volunteer Days
    ```

19. Select *Janisha Robinson* and change the font size to **28 pt**. Select the second line and change the font size to **18 pt**.

20. Click the text box border to select the entire object.

21. Choose **Home→Paragraph→Center** .

22. Choose **Drawing Tools→Format→Shape Styles→Shape Outline menu ▼** and choose **No Outline**.

23. Choose **Drawing Tools→Format→Shape Styles→Shape Fill menu ▼** and choose **White, Background 1, Darker 5%**.

24. If necessary, drag the text box by its border to center it between the margins.

25. Scroll down until the bottom of the page is visible.

26. Choose **Insert→Illustrations→Shapes** , and then choose **Text Box** .
    It should now appear in the Recently Used Shapes at the top of the gallery.

27. Draw a text box that is approximately **2 ½ inches wide and 1 inch high**, positioning it in the bottom-right corner, but within the 1-inch bottom and right-hand margins.

28. Type the following text:

    ```
    Presented by Kids for Change
    July 10, 2013
    ```

29. Click the border of the text box.

30. Choose **Drawing Tools→Format→Shape Styles→Shape Outline menu ▼** and choose **No Outline**.

31. Choose **Home→Font** and then choose **14 pt** from the Font Size drop-down list.

32. Resize the text box for the new font size.

33. With the text box selected, choose **Drawing Tools→Format→Shape Styles→Shape Fill menu ▼,** and then choose **White, Background 1, Darker 5%**.

Insert a SmartArt Object

34. Position the insertion point next to the last paragraph symbol.

35. Choose **Insert→Illustrations→SmartArt** , and then choose the **List** category in the left-hand pane.

36. Scroll down, choose **Vertical Chevron List**, and click **OK**.

Don't be concerned about the position of objects. You'll fix that shortly.

37. Click the tab on the left side of the graphic to open the **Type Your Text Here pane**.

The text pane may open on the right side of the image. You can resize the text pane like other objects by positioning the mouse pointer on the border and dragging when the mouse pointer appears as a double-headed arrow.

38. If necessary, resize the text pane until you can see all nine bullets.

39. Click and drag in the text pane to select the first six bullets, and then tap ⟨Delete⟩.

40. Type this text:

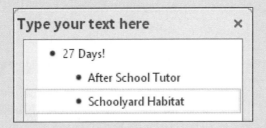

41. In the text pane, select the text for the first bullet.

42. Choose **Home→Font→Font Color** ⟨A⟩.

43. If the font color on the button face is red, click the button face. Otherwise, click the menu ▼ and choose **Red** in the Standard Colors section, and then close the **Type Your Text Here pane**.

44. Position the mouse pointer on the sizing handle in the bottom-right corner of the graphic. When the mouse pointer changes to a double-headed arrow, drag up and to the left until the image is approximately **3½ inches wide** and **1 inch tall**.

The graphic should pop up to the first page when you resize it. If necessary, continue resizing until it moves to the first page.

45. With the object selected, click the **Layout Options smart tag** next to it and choose **Top and Bottom** text wrapping.

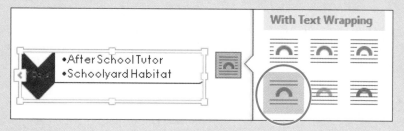

The smart tag can be a little shy at times. You may need to deselect and then reselect the image to encourage the smart tag to appear. Applying text wrapping allows you to freely position the SmartArt graphic on the page.

46. If necessary, drag both the SmartArt image and the bottom text box close to the bottom of the page.

47. Press ⎡Shift⎤ and click the bottom text box. (Both images should display handles.)

48. Choose **Drawing Tools→Format→Arrange→Align Objects** ⬚, and then choose **Align Top**.

49. Click in the document to deselect the images.

50. Click the **SmartArt image** and then click the border of the object with the bullets.
Handles should appear on the bulleted object.

51. Choose **SmartArt Tools→Format→Shape Styles→Shape Fill ▼ menu**, and then choose **White, Background 1, Darker 5%**.

52. Click in the document to deselect the object.

Apply a Page Color and a Page Border

53. Choose **Design→Page Background→Page Color** ⬚, and then choose **White, Background 1, Darker 5%**.

54. Choose **Design→Page Background→Page Borders** ⬚.

55. In the Borders and Shading dialog box, click the drop-down arrow in the **Art** field, scroll down, and choose the first row of stars. Click **OK**.

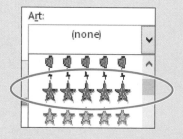

56. Make any sizing and positioning modifications you deem necessary.

57. If necessary, choose **Home→Paragraph→Show/Hide** ¶ to turn off formatting marks.

58. Save and close the certificate; exit **Word**.

59. Submit your final file based on the guidelines provided by your instructor.
To see examples of how your final file or files should look at the end of this exercise, go to the student resource center.

Create a Form

In this exercise, you will create a form that will be distributed to Kids for Change volunteers to make sure their information is current. You will use legacy form fields, including text-form fields, drop-down lists, and checkboxes, and you will use the Date Picker Content Control. You will use a Word table as the basis for the form.

Set Up the Form

1. Start **Word**. Open **WD09-R02-Volunteer** from your **WD2013 Lesson 09** folder and save it as `WD09-R02-Volunteer-[FirstInitialLastName]`.

2. Right-click the **Home** tab and choose **Customize the Ribbon**.

3. Place a checkmark in the **Developer** checkbox in the right-hand list and click **OK**.

4. If necessary, choose **Home→Paragraph→Show/Hide¶** to display formatting marks.

5. If necessary, choose **View→Show→Ruler** to display the ruler.

6. Position the insertion point in the first table cell and type this text:

   ```
   Contact·information¶
   Name¤
   ```

7. Check the ruler to make sure a **Left Tab** is in effect. If not, click the **Tab** box until the tab symbol looks like an uppercase L.

8. Click the ruler to place a tab at the **1¼-inch mark**.

9. Make sure the insertion point is next to *Name* in the second line of the cell, and then press Ctrl + Tab to position the insertion point at the tab.

Insert Form Fields

10. Choose **Developer→Controls→Legacy Tools** 🛠. Choose **Text Form Field** abl from the menu.

11. If the text field is not shaded, follow these steps. Otherwise, go to the next step.
    - Choose **Developer→Controls→Legacy Tools** 🛠.
    - Choose **Form Field Shading** 🖻.

12. Tap Enter, type **Primary phone**, and press Ctrl + Tab.

13. Insert another **Text Form Field** abl.

14. Tap Enter and type **Secondary phone**.

15. Press Ctrl + Tab to position the insertion point.

16. Insert another **Text Form Field** abl.

17. Set a tab on the ruler at the **2¼-inch mark** and then press Ctrl + Tab.

18. Type **Type** and then tap Spacebar twice.

19. Choose **Developer→Controls→Legacy Tools** ▦.

20. Choose **Drop-Down Form Field** ▦.

21. Tap [Enter] and type `Preferred contact method`.

22. Press [Ctrl]+[Tab] and insert another **Drop-Down Form Field** ▦.

23. Tap [Tab] to position the insertion point in the next cell.

24. Choose **Home→Paragraph→Align Right** ▤.

25. Choose **Developer→Controls→Date Picker Content Control** ▦ (not a legacy tool).

26. Position the insertion point in the first cell of the second row, type `Availability`, and tap [Enter].

27. Type `Preferred day` and set a tab on the ruler at the **1¼- inch mark**.

28. Press [Ctrl]+[Tab] to position the insertion point.

29. Insert a **Drop-Down Form Field** ▦.

Add Checkboxes and Complete the Form

30. Tap [Enter], type `Preferred time`, and press [Ctrl]+[Tab].

31. Type `Morning` and tap [Spacebar] twice.

32. Choose **Developer→Controls, Legacy Tools** ▦.

33. Choose **Check Box Form Field** ☑.

34. Tap [Spacebar] twice and type `Afternoon`.

35. Tap [Spacebar] twice, and then insert another **Check Box Form Field** ☑.

36. Tap [Tab] to move to the next table cell.

37. Complete the form as shown and using these guidelines:
    - Set a tab at the **4¾-inch mark**.
    - The first two lines contain **Drop-Down Form Fields** ▦.
    - The last line contains **Check Box Form Fields** ☑.
    - Apply spacing as shown in the illustration.

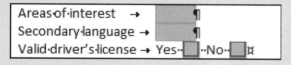

Apply Field Properties

38. Double-click the text field next to **Primary phone** in the first cell.

39. Change the Maximum Length field to **12** and click **OK**.

    This prevents users from typing too many characters for the phone number.

40. Double-click the text field next to **Secondary phone**, change the Maximum Length field to **12**, and click **OK**.

41. Double-click the drop-down field next to **Type**.

42. Type **Home** and click **Add** to place the first entry in the Items in the Drop-Down List field.

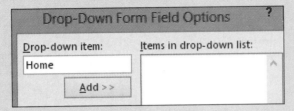

43. Follow the same process to add **Cell** and **Business** to the list; click **OK**.

44. Double-click the **Preferred contact** method drop-down field and add these items: **Email**, **Phone**. Click **OK**.

45. Tap Tab to position the insertion point in the next table cell.

46. Type **Click arrow; choose today's date**.

47. In the first cell of the second row, double-click the **Preferred day field** and add six days, **Monday** through **Saturday**, to the Items in Drop-Down List field.

48. Click **OK**.

49. In the second cell of the second row, double-click the **Areas of interest field** and add these items to the Items in Drop-Down List field:

   ■ **After School Tutor**
   ■ **Schoolyard Habitat**
   ■ **Recycling**
   ■ **Food Drive**

50. Click **OK**.

51. Double-click the **Secondary language field** and add these following items to the Items in Drop-Down List field:

   ■ **Spanish**
   ■ **Chinese**
   ■ **Vietnamese**
   ■ **Arabic**
   ■ **American Sign Language**

52. Click **OK**.

53. Choose **Home→Paragraph→Show/Hide ¶** to turn off formatting marks.

54. Choose **Developer→Controls→Legacy Tools**, and then choose **Form Field Shading**.

Protect and Use the Form

55. Choose **Developer→Protect→Restrict Editing** .

56. Make the choices shown at right in the Editing Restrictions area of the Restrict Editing task pane.

> **2. Editing restrictions**
> ☑ Allow only this type of editing in the document:
> [Filling in forms ▾]

57. Click **Yes, Start Enforcing Protection**, and then click **OK** to bypass using passwords.

58. If the Name field is not highlighted, click to the right of the word Name at about 1 ¼″ on the Ruler to display the highlight.

59. Type **Stella Harris** in the Name field and tap ⌷Tab⌷.

60. Type **712-555-1478** as the primary phone and tap ⌷Tab⌷ and type **712-555-9632** as the secondary phone.

61. Choose **Cell** from the Type drop-down list.

62. Choose **Phone** from the Preferred contact method drop-down list.

63. Tap ⌷Tab⌷ to position the insertion point in the next table cell.

64. Click the arrow, and then click **Today** to enter the current date.

65. Complete the second row as shown:

Availability			Areas of interest	Schoolyard Habitat	
Preferred day	Saturday		Secondary language	Vietnamese	
Preferred time	Morning ☐	Afternoon ☒	Valid driver's license	Yes ☒	No ☐

66. Click the **Stop Protection** button in the task pane then close it.

67. Right-click the **Home** tab and choose **Customize the Ribbon**.

68. Remove the checkmark from the Developer checkbox in the right-hand list and click **OK**.

69. Save and close your file; exit from **Word**.

70. Submit your final file based on guidelines provided by your instructor.

    To see examples of how your file or files should look at the end of this exercise, go to the student resource center.

Create a Flyer and a Form

In this exercise, you will create a flyer using graphic shapes and SmartArt. You will format and size the images, and add a page background color and a page border. You will also create, protect, and fill in a form.

Work with Shapes

Kids for Change is partnering with a local charity that collects clothing and household products for people with developmental disabilities. One of the members is creating a flyer to help in the collection process.

1. Start **Word**. Open **WD09-R03-Donations** from your **WD2013 Lesson 09** folder and save it as `WD09-R03-Donations-[FirstInitialLastName]`.

2. If necessary, choose **Home→Paragraph→Show/Hide** ¶ to display formatting marks.

3. If necessary, choose **View→Show→Ruler** to display the ruler.

4. Check that the box at the left side of the ruler is displaying a **Left Tab**. If not, click the **Tab box** until the symbol looks like an uppercase L.

5. Choose **Insert→Illustrations→Shapes** ⬡, and then choose **Wave** in the Stars and Banners category.

6. Starting at the left margin, drag the crosshair mouse pointer to the right until the image is about **6 inches wide** and down until it is about **2 inches tall**.

7. Type this text on two separate lines:

   `We need your gently used clothing, shoes, and household items!`
   `Donating is as easy as 1-2-3!`

Format the Shape

8. Click the border of the object to select it.

9. Choose **Home→Font** and choose **16 pt** from the Font Size list.

10. If necessary, drag the shape until it is just below the clip art image and centered between the margins.

11. With the object selected, choose **Drawing Tools→Format→Shape Styles→Shape Fill menu ▼** and choose **Blue, Accent 1, Darker 25%**.

Insert a SmartArt Image

12. Position the insertion point on the second blank line below the Shape.

13. Choose **Insert→Illustration→SmartArt** 📄, and then choose **List** in the left-hand pane

14. Choose **Vertical Curved List** and click **OK**.

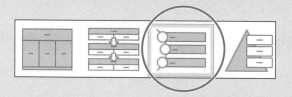

Don't be concerned about the position and size of the object. You'll fix that shortly.

15. Click the tab on the left side of the graphic to display the **Type Your Text Here** box.

16. Enter this text, and then close the text pane.

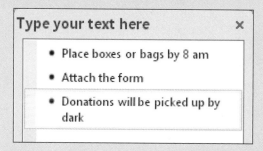

17. Place the mouse pointer in the bottom-center handle of the SmartArt object and drag up until the image is about **2 inches tall**.

18. Position the mouse pointer on the right-hand sizing handle and drag left until the right edge is close to the word *dark* in the last line.

19. With the object selected, click the **Layout Options smart tag** and choose **Top and Bottom** text wrapping.

Now you can move the image freely on the page.

20. Drag the **SmartArt image** close to the bottom of the Wave Shape and center it between the margins.

Apply a SmartArt Style

21. If necessary, select the image, and then click the border of the first rectangle.

Handles should appear around the rectangle.

22. Press ⟨Shift⟩ and click the other two rectangles.

Handles should now appear around all three rectangles.

23. Choose **SmartArt Tools→Format→Shape Styles→Shape Fill menu ▼,** and then choose **Blue, Accent 1, Darker 25%**.

Add a Page Color and a Page Border

24. Click in the document to deselect the **SmartArt image**.

25. Choose **Design→Page Background→Page Color** 🖼, and then choose **Blue, Accent, Lighter 60%**.

26. Choose **Design→Page Background, Page Borders** 🗋. In the **Art** field, choose the border shown.

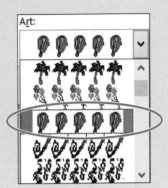

27. Click **OK**. Adjust the size and position of any objects you deem necessary.

Create a Form

28. Delete five paragraph symbols below the SmartArt image to place the table at the bottom of the first page.

29. Right-click the **Home** tab and choose **Customize the Ribbon**.

30. Place a checkmark in the **Developer** checkbox in the right-hand list and click **OK**.

31. Position the insertion point in the first table cell.

32. Place a tab on the ruler at the **1¼-inch mark**.

33. Type **Name** and press ⎵Ctrl⎵ + ⎵Tab⎵ to position the insertion point.

34. Choose **Developer→Controls→Legacy Tools→Text Form Field** 🔘.

35. Tap ⎵Enter⎵ and then type **Street address**.

36. Press ⎵Ctrl⎵ + ⎵Tab⎵ to position the insertion point.

37. Insert another **Text Form Field** 🔘.

38. Tap ⎵Tab⎵ to position the insertion point in the next table cell.

39. Place a tab on the ruler at the **2-inch mark** and type **What day do you prefer?**

40. Press ⎵Ctrl⎵ + ⎵Tab⎵ to position the insertion point.

41. Choose **Developer→Controls→Legacy Tools→Drop-Down Form Field** 🔲.

42. Tap ⎵Enter⎵ and type **What time do you prefer?**

    If tapping ⎵Enter⎵ *placed part of the table on a second page, resize a graphic image until everything fits on one page.*

43. Press ⎵Ctrl⎵ + ⎵Tab⎵ to position the insertion point, type **AM**, and tap ⎵Spacebar⎵ twice.

44. Choose **Developer→Controls→Legacy Tools→Checkbox Form Field** ☑.

45. Tap ⎵Spacebar twice, type **PM**, and tap ⎵Spacebar twice.

46. Choose **Developer→Controls→Legacy Tools→Checkbox Form Field** ☑.

Apply a Field Property

47. Double-click the field to the right of *What day do you prefer?* to open the **Drop-Down Form Fields dialog box**.

48. Type **Monday** in the Drop-Down Item field and click **Add** to place the item in the **Items in Drop-Down List field**.

49. Use the same process to add the days **Tuesday** through **Saturday** to the list; click **OK**.

50. Choose **Home→Paragraph→Show/Hide** ¶ to turn off formatting marks.

51. Choose **Developer→Controls→Legacy Tools→Form Field Shading** 🔲 to turn off the feature.

Protect and Use the Form

52. Choose **Developer→Protect→Restrict Editing** 🔒.

53. Make the choices shown at right in the Editing Restrictions area of the Restrict Editing task pane.

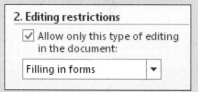

54. Click **Yes, Start Enforcing Protection**, and then click **OK** to bypass using a password.

55. If the *Name* field is not highlighted, click to the right of it to display the highlight.

56. Type **Janice Johnson** in the **Name** field.

57. Tap Tab and type **123 Cherry Blossom Lane**.

58. Tap Tab and choose **Wednesday** from the drop-down field.

59. Click the **AM** checkbox

60. Click the **Stop Protection** button in the task pane, and then close it.

61. Save and close your file; exit **Word**.

62. Submit your final file based on guidelines provided by your instructor.

Apply Your Skills

Create a Flyer

In this exercise, you will create a flyer, and add and format a shape and a SmartArt image. You will then add a page background color and a page border.

Insert and Format a Shape and Align Objects

1. Start **Word**. Open **WD09-A01-CarRental** from your **WD2013 Lesson 09** folder and save it as `WD09-A01-CarRental-[FirstInitialLastName]`.

2. If necessary, turn on formatting marks and the ruler.

3. Choose the **Double Wave** shape.

4. About a half-inch below the picture, draw the shape about **4½ inches wide** and **1 inch tall**.

5. Type `Book now!` in the shape. Change the font size to **36 pt** and adjust the shape size as necessary.

6. Change the **Shape Fill** color to **Tan, Background 2, Darker 50%**.

7. Select the WordArt heading, the picture, and the Double Wave Shape at the same time.

8. Use the contextual **Format** tab and the **Align Objects** ▣ feature to center-align the objects.

Insert, Apply a Style to, and Format a SmartArt Image

9. Position the insertion point on the first blank line below the shape.

10. Insert the **Table List SmartArt graphic** (in the List category) shown here.

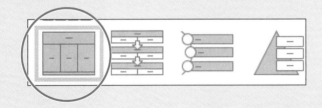

11. Open the **Type Your Text Here pane** and type the text shown. When finished, close the text pane.

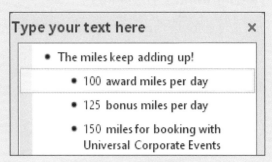

12. Using the SmartArt Styles gallery on the contextual Design tab, apply the 3-D **Inset** style.

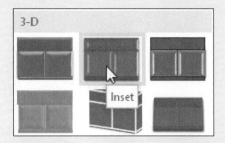

13. Select the individual objects within the SmartArt Graphic—the top row, the thin bottom row, and the three squares in between.

14. Change the **Shape Fill** color to **Tan, Background 2, Darker 50%**.

15. Use the bottom-center sizing handle to change the height of the image to about **2 inches**. It should now fit on the first page. If not, reduce the height until it does.

16. Use the **Layout Options smart tag** to change the text wrapping to **Top and Bottom**.

17. If necessary, drag the SmartArt image up to page 1 and center it between the margins.

18. Delete enough paragraph symbols at the bottom of the page to reduce the document to one page.

Add a Page Color and a Page Border

19. Change the **Page Color** to **Tan, Background 2, Darker 25%**.

20. Apply the border style shown here. The color is **Tan, Background 2, Darker 50%**.

21. Turn off formatting marks.

22. Save and close your file; exit **Word**.

23. Submit your final file based on guidelines provided by your instructor.

    To see examples of how your final file or files should look at the end of this exercise, go to the student resource center.

APPLY YOUR SKILLS WD09-A02

Create a Trip-Planning Form

In this exercise, you will create a form containing checkboxes, text fields, and a drop-down list. You will add field properties, and then you will protect the form and fill it in.

Set up a Form and Insert Form Fields

1. Start **Word**. Open **WD09-A02-CorpTravel** from your **WD2013 Lesson 09** folder and save it as **WD09-A02-CorpTravel-[FirstInitialLastName]**.

2. If necessary, display formatting marks, the ruler, and the Developer tab.

3. Position the insertion point in the first table cell.

4. Follow these guidelines to enter the information shown in the following illustration.
   - Apply spacing as shown in the illustration.
   - Use the **Legacy Tools Check Box Form Fields**.
   - Space twice after each checkbox and type the labels shown.
   - The checkboxes in the second column are aligned on left tabs set at **2½ inches**.

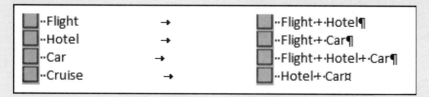

5. Position the insertion point in the second table row, below the word *Flight*.

6. Follow these guidelines to enter the data shown in the following illustration.
   - Apply spacing as shown.
   - In the first row of information, set left tabs at **2** and **4** inches; use **Legacy Tools' Check Box Form Fields**.
   - In the second row, use the tab set at **2** inches; use **Legacy Tools' Text Form Fields**.
   - In the third row, leave the tab at 2 inches in place; use **Legacy Tools' Text Form Fields**.
   - In the last row, insert a **Legacy Tools' Drop-Down Form Field**.

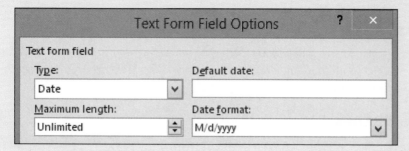

Apply Field Properties

7. Apply the field properties shown to the **Departure date** and **Return date** fields.

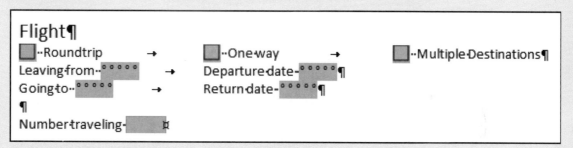

8. Add the numbers **1 - 9** to the **Drop-Down Form Field** at the bottom of the form.

Protect and Complete the Form

9. If necessary, turn off formatting marks and **Form Field Shading** .

10. Apply the **Editing Restrictions** as shown.

> **2. Editing restrictions**
> ☑ Allow only this type of editing in the document:
>
> | Filling in forms | ▼ |

11. Start protecting the form; bypass using a password.

12. Fill in the form using the data and choices shown here.

☐ Flight   ☐ Flight + Hotel
☐ Hotel   ☐ Flight + Car
☐ Car   ☒ Flight + Hotel + Car
☐ Cruise   ☐ Hotel + Car

Flight
☐ Roundtrip   ☐ One way   ☒ Multiple Destinations
Leaving from New York City   Departure date 8/13/2013
Going to London   Return date 8/20/2013

Number traveling 3

13. Stop protection and close the **Restrict Editing task pane**.

14. Save and close your file; exit **Word**.

15. Submit your final file based on guidelines provided by your instructor.

    To see examples of how your final file or files should look at the end of this exercise, go to the student resource center.

Create a Flyer and a Form

In this exercise, you will insert shapes and a SmartArt graphic. Then you will set up a form in a table and use text fields, checkboxes, a drop-down list, and the Date Picker Content Control. Finally, you will add a page color and a page border.

Work with Shapes

1. Start **Word**. Open **WD09-A03-Universal** from your **WD2013 Lesson 09** folder and save it as WD09-A03-Universal-[FirstInitialLastName].

2. If necessary, display formatting marks and turn on the ruler.

3. Turn on **Form Field Shading** .

4. Choose the **Horizontal Scroll** shape.

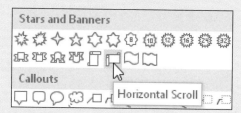

5. Draw the shape at the top of the document, sizing it at the width of the page but between the margins and about **1½ inches tall**.

6. Type `Universal Corporate Events` in the shape and change the font size to **26 pt**.

7. Insert a text box shape about a half-inch below the top shape, making it about **3½ inches wide** and **½ inch tall**.

8. Type `Services We Offer` in the box and change the font size to **26 pt**.

9. Apply the **Text Effect** Ⓐ shown here.

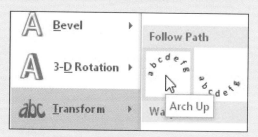

10. Apply the Text Fill color in the fifth column, **Dark Red, Accent 1, Darker 25%**.

11. Use **Shape Outline** to remove the outline.

12. Apply the **Shape Fill** color in the first column, **White, Background 1, Darker 15%**.

13. Position the insertion point on the second blank line below the text box.

Insert and Format a SmartArt Graphic

14. Insert the **Vertical Box List** SmartArt graphic.

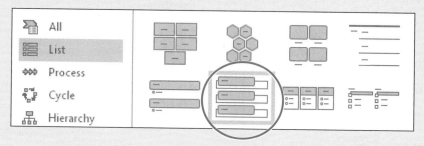

15. Open the **Type Your Text Here pane** and enter this text:

16. Close the text pane.

17. Select the four rounded rectangles within the SmartArt Shape and apply italics.

Apply a Page Color and a Page Border

18. Apply the third page color in the first column, **White, Background 1, Darker 15%**.

19. Apply the page border shown here. The color is **Dark Red, Accent 1, Darker 25%**.

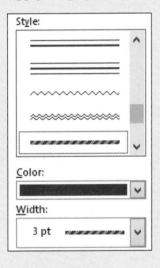

Set Up a Form

20. Insert a **2x2 table** about a half-inch below the SmartArt image.

21. On the **Layout** tab, change the top and bottom cell margins to **0.08**.

22. Position the insertion point in the first table cell.

23. Set a left tab at the **¾-inch mark** on the ruler and enter the information shown, inserting the **Legacy Tools' Text Form Fields** where indicated.

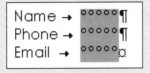

24. In the second cell of the first row, insert the **Date Picker Content Control**  right-aligned.

25. Enter the information shown in the following illustration in the first cell of the second row using these guidelines:

- Apply spacing as shown.
- Place a **left tab** at the **1½-inch mark** on the ruler.
- Insert a **Drop-Down Form Field** below Destination.
- Use **Check Box Form Fields** for the services.

26. Enter the information shown in the following illustration in the last table cell using these guidelines:

- Apply spacing as shown.
- Set a **left tab** at the **4¾-inch mark** on the ruler.
- Use **Text Form Fields**.

Resize and reposition graphic images and delete paragraph symbols as necessary to fit everything on one page.

Apply Field Properties

27. Click the **Date Picker Content Control** in the second cell of the first row and type **Click arrow; choose today's date.**

28. In the first cell of the second row, add these destinations to the Drop-Down Form Field: **Samoa**, **Fiji**, **Tahiti**, **Tonga**.

29. Apply these properties to the two text fields in the last cell.

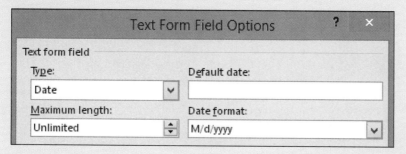

Protect and Use the Form

30. If necessary, turn off formatting marks and **Form Field Shading** 🄰.

31. Apply the Editing Restrictions as shown in the following illustration.

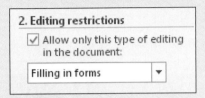

32. Fill in the form with the information shown, using the current date in the second cell of the first row. Bypass setting a password.

Name Ned Bennett Phone 712-555-4563 Email Ned@Yahoo.com	2/16/2013

Destination   Services
Tonga   ☒ Air
                              ☒ Hotel
                              ☐ Car
	Departure date 10/10/2013
	Return date 10/21/2013

33. Stop protection and close the **Restrict Editing task pane**.

34. Save and close your file; exit **Word**.

35. Submit your final file based on guidelines provided by your instructor.

Extend Your Skills

In the course of working through the Extend Your Skills exercises, you will think critically as you use the skills taught in the lesson to complete the assigned projects. To evaluate your mastery and completion of the exercises, your instructor may use a rubric, with which more points are allotted according to performance characteristics. (The more you do, the more you earn!) Ask your instructor how your work will be evaluated.

WD09-E01 That's the Way I See It

As the owner of a small online business, you want to promote a new product you are carrying. Start a new Word document and save it in your **WD2013 Lesson 09** folder as **WD09-E01-NewProd-[FirstInitialLastName]**. Create a brochure using shapes and SmartArt graphics to announce the product. Add the formatting of your choice to the graphic images. Add a page background color and page border to the brochure. Add a second page that contains a discount voucher form. Include text fields where customers will enter their contact information, include a drop-down list where they can choose the type of credit card they will use, and include at least three checkboxes where customers can specify their preferred shipping method. Apply appropriate field properties. Protect the form, and then fill it in with data of your choice. Finally, unprotect the form.

You will be evaluated based on the inclusion of all elements specified, your ability to follow directions, your ability to apply newly learned skills to a real-world situation, your creativity, and the relevance of your topic and/or data choice(s). Submit your final file based on the guidelines provided by your instructor.

WD09-E02 Be Your Own Boss

As the owner of Blue Jean Landscaping, you're hoping to increase sales as your customers get ready to spruce up their gardens with spring plants. Start a new Word document and save it to your **WD2013 Lesson 09** folder as **WD09-E02-Spring-[FirstInitialLastName]**. Create a flyer using shapes and SmartArt graphics with upbeat verbiage about spring gardening. Size and format the graphics based on your personal preferences. Add a survey form at the bottom of the flyer that includes checkboxes so customers can indicate the products they are interested in, such as shrubs, flowers, potting soil, and so forth. Conduct an online search for eco-friendly fertilizers. Include a drop-down list of at least three different fertilizers so customers can indicate their preference. Include a text-form field where customers can comment about your company's service. Limit the amount of text they can type to 200 characters. Apply other form properties as appropriate. Protect the form and then fill it in with data of your choice. Finally, unprotect the form.

You will be evaluated based on the inclusion of all elements specified, your ability to follow directions, your ability to apply newly learned skills to a real-world situation, your creativity, and your demonstration of an entrepreneurial spirit. Submit your final file based on the guidelines provided by your instructor.

Transfer Your Skills

In the course of working through the Transfer Your Skills exercises, you will use critical-thinking and creativity skills to complete the assigned projects using skills taught in the lesson. To evaluate your mastery and completion of the exercises, your instructor may use a rubric, with which more points are allotted according to performance characteristics. (The more you do, the more you earn!) Ask your instructor how your work will be evaluated.

WD09-T01 Use the Web as a Learning Tool

Throughout this book, you will be provided with an opportunity to use the Internet as a learning tool by completing WebQuests. According to the original creators of WebQuests, as described on their website (WebQuest.org), a WebQuest is "an inquiry-oriented activity in which most or all of the information used by learners is drawn from the web." To complete the WebQuest projects in this book, navigate to the student resource center and choose the WebQuest for the lesson on which you are currently working. The subject of each WebQuest will be relevant to the material found in the lesson.

WebQuest Subject: Creating a well-designed brochure.

Submit your final file(s) based on the guidelines provided by your instructor.

WD09-T02 Demonstrate Proficiency

Stormy BBQ is expanding to include a catering department! You have been asked to create a brochure announcing this new venture. Start a new Word document and save it in your **WD2013 Lesson 09** folder as **WD09-T02-Catering-[FirstInitialLastName]**. Include shapes and SmartArt graphics promoting the services Stormy BBQ will offer. Add a second page containing a form that customers can use for placing catering orders. It should include contact information and a drop-down list where they can choose the type of event (e.g., birthday, wedding, corporate luncheon). Include two columns of checkboxes with at least three items per column so customers can choose BBQ items, such as brisket and ribs, in the first column, and side-dish items, such as baked beans and coleslaw, in the second column. Apply form properties as appropriate. Include a background color and page border. And, because this brochure will need approval before being sent out, include a watermark indicating the document is in Draft mode.

Submit your final file based on the guidelines provided by your instructor.

Index

Notes

Notes

Notes

Notes

Notes

Notes

Notes

Notes

Notes

Notes

Notes

Notes

Notes

Notes